128
WAT
#6492

Watson, Jeffrey A.
    Looking beyond.

$5.95

LOOKING

JEFFREY A. WATSON

This book is designed for your personal reading pleasure and profit.

It is also designed for group study. A Leader's Guide with helps and hints for teachers and with visual aids (Victor Multiuse Transparency Masters) is available from your local bookstore or from the publisher.

BEYOND

#6492

VICTOR BOOKS

A DIVISION OF SCRIPTURE PRESS PUBLICATIONS INC.
USA CANADA ENGLAND

Most Scripture taken from the *New American Standard Bible*, © the Lockman Foundation 1960, 1962, 1963, 1968, 1971, 1972, 1973, 1975, 1977. Used by permission. Other quotations are from the *King James Version* (KJV).

Recommended Dewey Decimal Classification: 236.1
Suggested Subject Heading: DOCTRINAL THEOLOGY OF DEATH
Library of Congress Catalog Card Number: 85-62709
ISBN: 0-89693-155-2

© 1986 by SP Publications, Inc.

CONTENTS

This book is dedicated to Mr. Gerald Wayne Root (1954-84)—friend, Christian brother, courageous soldier in his fights against cancer and leukemia, husband, father of three . . . and newly in the presence of the Lord.

JEFF AND NANCY WATSON

PREFACE

You are about to follow the lead of Moses, who wrote, "So teach us to number our days, that we may apply our hearts unto wisdom" (Ps. 90:12, KJV). As Moses penned these words, he was reflecting on the Israelites' death-ridden wilderness journey from Egypt. He could picture a generation of his companions fading like flowers or withering like grass under the scorching desert sun.

As Moses' people first heard these words, they were challenged to live their lives as opportunities for personal growth and spiritual wisdom. His perspective likewise challenges us today to be aware that our earthly time clocks are running. He is encouraging us centuries later to avoid foolish ways of living, and to live wisely, skillfully, and according to God's pattern.

Looking Beyond offers an overview of the Bible's teachings on the future, aging, suffering, grief, death, and the afterlife. I trust this book will influence you, your family, and your church toward healthy, spiritual thinking and living. I pray with Moses that God would "teach us to number our days that we may apply our hearts unto wisdom."

JEFFREY A. WATSON

PART ONE

LOOKING AT DEATH

1

The Origin and Destiny of Death

A minister who had been given no preparation for dealing with death was assigned to his first church.[1] As soon as he arrived, the young pastor faced a difficult test: an 11-year-old boy from the church died suddenly of a juvenile heart attack.

At the graveside the mother was so distraught that she jumped into the grave to embrace the coffin of her only son. After she was helped back out, she faced the minister. As everyone watched, she looked him straight in the eye and asked, "Why? Why did this happen?"

The new pastor stood dumbfounded. He thought of answering, "Heart attack," but that was the medical answer and she already knew it. She was really asking, "Why does death happen? Why must we die? How did we get ourselves into this dilemma?"

Why Does Death Happen?

That bereaved mother's question, and others like it, are on the minds of many people today. Where did death come from? Has it always been with us? Who's in charge of life and death? Will death always be such an unrelenting foe?

For each question, modern man poses many answers. Let's suppose that we stop a few dozen people on the street and tell them the mother's story of losing her 11-year-old son. Then we ask, "Why does death happen, where does death come from,

11

and where is it going?" After our survey is over, our list might include answers from the following:

The Secularist: "Well, even the death of an 11-year-old comes by random biological chance. You take your chances; when the old machine quits, it quits. That's the end. I guess we evolved through the survival of the fittest, and when we stop being healthy enough to compete with our environment, we die—we become personally extinct."

The Liberal Churchman: "It is certainly a tragedy when anybody dies. But the positive side is that this boy doesn't have any more hell to live through. Hell is the bad problems we go through in life, you know. Maybe this child and his family would have experienced more pain had he lived. God accepts all of us; He is love. This idea of sin and judgment is archaic, so the mother has nothing to worry about. Maybe she should get a prescription sedative or go to a psychiatrist to get rid of her grief."

The Eastern Mystic: "I think the mother shouldn't be so uptight. I mean, life and death have been an infinite circle forever. Her son has lived before and will live again—maybe as a plant, an animal, or another person. There's always the possibility that this child only had a little bit of *karma* to work off—a little bit of worldliness to purge from his previous life. That might be why he died early; he was done working off his karma. Maybe he has united with cosmic consciousness already. Nothing better than that! To be free of the body is the greatest blessing."

The Roman Catholic: "It's hard for me to feel anything definite about this, since I don't know whether the boy was Catholic. If I knew he had been baptized and had a Catholic funeral, I'd feel better. I sure hope he was given last rites by a priest. Even if he wasn't Catholic, his Catholic relatives and friends could hold a mass for him and say prayers to the saints for him. Even if he was an atheist, he certainly didn't go to hell—he was too young to commit those kinds of sins. I know he's not an infant, so he didn't go to limbo. But I could be 99 percent sure he's in purgatory. That's hopeful, because God gives all of us a second chance there."

Most people desperately need to know God's truth about life and death. To be ignorant of the Bible's teachings on death is to risk spiritual and emotional catastrophe. As we examine Scripture we can more firmly grasp our own faith—and respond more skillfully to people like that bereaved mother who are asking legitimate questions and feeling genuine pain.

Death: Through Man, from God

In the beginning, God caused all life to exist. Humans, animals, and plants all came into existence at the command of the Creator (Gen. 1:1-27; 2:7; 2:19). In this world of new life, God warned that rebellion against Him would result in death (2:17). Life was fragile. It could be taken away.

Soon Satan posed a deceptive question to man: Could man avoid dying even if he disobeyed God? (3:4) Temptation turned to action and the divine consequence of death was reaffirmed (3:19). Man and woman, now alienated from their Creator, would find their world plagued by death. The man, whose lot it was to produce life-maintaining crops, would find the soil stubborn and the weeds threatening (3:17-19). The woman, who was to produce offspring to perpetuate the race, would find childbirth painful (3:16).

Adam and Eve would eventually die (5:5), having been banished from the life-giving tree (3:22-24). Though it was 930 years before Adam's life ended, his story confirmed the warning of God that human rebellion against the divine Creator results in death. The rebellion of this first couple resulted not only in their own deaths, but in the inevitable process of death for the whole human race.

There were many participants in that first drama of defiance, but it was God who chose death as the necessary result of sin. Death did not "sneak by" God in secret. It did not rage out of control or surprise Him. It was not a creation of Satan or "chance." God chose death as the divinely logical and appropriate consequence of sin (Rom. 5:12, 19; 6:22-23; 8:19-22; 1 Cor. 15:21-22). Though a criminal is responsible for his actions, the court is responsible for his sentence.

God instituted the inevitable, regular process of death. Now when a man dies, he "goes the way of all the earth" (Josh. 23:14; 1 Kings 2:1-2). Death does not come to an individual because some cruel and malign force has attacked him, as ancient Israel's neighbors thought. Death does not come because random biological chance has singled out a person's body for destruction, as modern secular thinkers suggest. Instead, physical death is a natural and regular process which God introduced and now superintends.

Being Realistic about Death

Stan was a typical middle-aged suburbanite, locked in the urban hustle but hungry for the quiet of the mountains and the open blue sky. Yet here we stood, not fishing in a mountain stream but huddled in a hospital emergency room. We were watching helplessly as Stan's wife grimaced in pain; she had been rushed to the hospital after collapsing in a grocery store.

Her diagnosis was undecided, but Stan's problem was obvious. He was coming unglued. Anxiety over what might happen to his wife turned his usually calm soul into a hurricane. As he thought about how horrible life would be without her, he too grimaced in pain.

Most people saw Stan as a calm, strong, logical man. A scientist, he certainly knew that the cycle of life included aging, illness, and death. But he strictly avoided all talk of those subjects, denying that these realities would ever touch him or the people he loved most. Stan "knew," for example, that he didn't need doctors. Even now he had a discolored growth on his arm which he had steadfastly refused to have biopsied.

As it turned out, his wife's medical problem would eventually be diagnosed and remedied. She would return home, and Stan would return to his "calm side"—at least until the next emergency.

Stan wraps himself in a tight blanket of denial most of the time. But we don't have to. Because God has complete control over death, we should have a balanced realism about the end of life. Old age can be valued and honored despite the physical deterioration it brings (Ecc. 3:2; Gen. 25:8; Prov. 16:31). Death can be seen as normal even though God has sometimes demonstrated His ability to sponsor life extension, resuscitation, resurrection, and miraculous ascension. Death is normal and under the unique control of God.

God Controls Life and Death Now

In Hannah's prayer of 1 Samuel 2:1-10, the Lord is seen as controlling every positive and negative experience of life. He not only permits a godly woman to be barren of children for years, but allows her to give birth in her old age. He not only allows evil to exist, but brings justice to bear on the corrupt. In a concise pair of poetic lines, Hannah describes God as being totally in control of life and death: "The Lord kills and makes alive; He brings down to sheol and raises up" (1 Sam. 2:6). He determines who lives and who dies, who comes close to death through physical illness and danger, and who rebounds to renewed life.

Life before Death

Throughout the Scriptures many facets of God's supremacy over life and death are detailed. For instance, we need not fear mortal men, but rather the immortal God (Isa. 51:12-13). Jesus is the total authority over death and hell (Rev. 1:17-18). We read of God's involvement with our births (Deut. 32:18), our urgent prayers for life (Heb. 5:7), the preservation of life (2 Sam. 14:14), and the spiritual dimensions of life and death (John 5:24; 8:21; Rom. 7:10, 24; 8:6; 1 John 3:14).

Though the Bible uses many theological descriptions of death, it is not without emotional perspectives as well. Death is understood as having a painful impact on people and on the society they live in. This is especially true when death comes to an infant or child, to one who is without an heir, through suicide, or through divine judgment. Yet in addition to death's negative qualities, Scripture associates many positive qualities with the end of earthly life. There are positive qualities in the afterlife such as joy (Ps. 16:9-11), a good reputation (Prov. 10:7), motivation to wisdom (Ps. 90:12-14), relief from misery (Job 3:11-19), and reunion (Gen. 49:29), for example.

Life after Death

The Lord not only controls how and when we die (Deut. 31:14; Ecc. 8:8), but He determines what happens to us *after* we die (Dan. 12:2-3; Matt. 25:31-46; John 8:51-53).

Concepts of Afterlife		
One-way destiny	All people suffer the same fate	Extinction/Rein-carnation/Uncon-ditional accep-tance by God
Two-way destiny	People are divided accord-ing to accep-tance or rejection of Christ	Heaven or hell
Three-way destiny	People are divided according to religions, beliefs, and personal good-ness vs. evil	Heaven or purgatory or hell

Concerning this afterlife, the Bible teaches that God allows one of two destinies for people—heaven or hell. There is no biblical support for a single destiny for the whole human race. There is also no biblical support for a three-way, middle-ground destiny where people are offered a chance to purge their wrongs and ascend to heaven.[2] It is only through genuine trust in the righteous life and death of Jesus Christ that we secure much-needed forgiveness. This Christ-centered forgiveness permits us to spend eternity with God in heaven (John 5:24; 17:3; Rom. 6:23; 10:9, 13).

Many people do not believe biblical concepts of life after death. They either ignore biblical teaching or inappropriately redefine biblical terms. Such people commonly redefine heaven and hell as the good and bad experiences of earthly life. Others believe in some form of afterlife, but try to prepare for it in unbiblical ways. Rather than grounding their faith in Jesus Christ, they depend on religious faithfulness, good luck, relative morality, asceticism, magic, or the intervention of saints to earn them a good destiny.

Can You Know for Sure?

A few years ago I was part of a missionary team on the island of Cyprus in the Mediterranean Sea. We ministered mostly in villages, camps, and churches, but one day went sightseeing at a monastery—the Greek Orthodox monastery of the Apostle Barnabas. The priests we met there were elderly men who had large beards, gray hair, and black robes. Their lives and religious service were focused on painting icons—gilded oil paintings of religious figures. These icons were the worship images for thousands of Greek Orthodox pilgrims who came each year to the monastery.

After talking with these men for some time and after presenting Gospel literature to them in modern Greek, a local missionary asked two key questions: "Are you certain that you will go to heaven when you die? If you are certain, then in what are you placing your spiritual confidence?"

Their answer struck and discouraged us. "Well, we hope we'll go to heaven when we die," they said. "After all, we've spent our whole lives in this place, painting these icons. If that is not enough, nothing is!"

How sad it was to see these men being faithful to their religion, trusting in their good works for eternal salvation. Like so many people today, they believed that death would come and that heaven was an eternal possibility. But they groped blindly, unable to connect the problem of their sin to the death of Christ. They didn't see that faith in Jesus Christ was the sole assurance for eternal life.

Two Lifestyles, Two Afterlives

People who center their faith and lives in Christ have changed natures (2 Cor. 5:17). They grow in the values that represent their life commitments (Col. 3:1-4). They are attracted to others whose lives are also genuinely rooted in Christ (1 John 3:14). As they grow, they develop traits such as love, conscience, and truthfulness (John 13:35; 14:15; 1 Cor. 2:10, 12-

17

16; 1 John 1:6-10; 2:4, 9). This pattern of Christ-centered spiritual life touches off a process which will not end at physical death (Phil. 1:6). It will grow beyond and through death, with God's presence as its ultimate destination.

By contrast, people who live self-righteously and for self-gratification are alienating themselves from Christ-centeredness. Their natures, values, actions, and companionship patterns run counter to a heaven-destined life. If by accident these people ended up in heaven without being converted to Christ, they would find heaven to be hellish for them. Their course, if it continues without repentance, will allow their spiritual void to be intensified for eternity.

Maury is a young man who seems bent on the latter course. An unusually handsome young man, he could have been a gifted athlete too if only he'd been self-disciplined. He could have gone to college; his IQ is well above average, and he used to show academic promise whenever he set his mind to a task. But he lacks self-control and purpose.

Maury was always interested mainly in fun and thrills; in time his thirst for drugs and sexual exploits became unquenchable. He began to spend most of his time with older guys who lived for fast cars, racial violence, and occasional crime. Maury's motto became, "Live hard and die young." The last time I saw him he was fulfilling his motto. After a nearly fatal heroin overdose, he was walking with a cane and slurring his speech. Worse yet, he was awaiting prosecution for shooting someone in a fight. He was living hard, all right, and probably will die young—unless he turns to Christ.

Each of us, Maury included, must prepare to stand before God. And each true believer must seek to communicate the Gospel to others in order to offer them the opportunity to prepare. Once the books have been opened and the judgment made, God will seal our chosen destinies for eternity (Rev. 20:12-15; 22:11-15).

These two destinies are reflected in the two resurrections to which the Bible refers. These resurrections will unite one's immaterial spirit with a revitalized body. The first is a "resurrection to life," also called the first resurrection (1 Cor. 15:20-24; Luke 14:13-14; John 5:28-29; Rev. 20:5-6). This God-approved, blessed occurrence begins with the resurrection of

Christ and the rapture of the church (1 Cor. 15:22-23; 1 Thes. 4:16). It culminates in the raising of all Old Testament believers and tribulation martyrs before the 1,000-year reign of Christ on earth (Dan. 12:2; Isa. 26:19; Rev. 20:3-5). The second is a "resurrection to damnation," also called the last resurrection (John 5:29; Rev. 20:11-14). This event follows the 1,000-year rule of Christ. The unrighteous dead who have not been cleansed by the blood of Christ shall be raised, sentenced, and judged for eternity.

The Choices

Will you spend the remainder of your days in terror and doubt? Or will you recognize that God has introduced death and controls it wisely? God has laid out two distinct alternatives for your eternal destiny. Will you reject His gift of eternal life through Jesus Christ? Will you choose an eternity of separation from God? Or will you reach out to that offer of kindness made through the saving death and resurrection of our Saviour?

Two Christian men were in a boating accident. As the two were plunged into the dark, icy waters of the Atlantic, they fought against fear, currents, and frigid temperatures. When the older man could no longer struggle, he began to float out to sea. As the younger man kept struggling to survive, he could hear the broken lines of familiar hymns sung by his dying friend. That friend died singing hymns, accepting his death, and at eternal peace with God. Long before the Coast Guard had pulled the icy corpse from the water, a warm embrace by a loving Saviour had welcomed that man home.

There is good news in the Bible. God controls life and death; death is not some arbitrary mystery or gruesome ghost lurking behind its unsuspecting victims. Because God has conquered death (1 Cor. 15:25-26, 53-55; John 11:26; 1 Tim. 6:16), we have His promise that physical death will end (Rev. 20:14; 21:4; Isa. 25:8). As the grain of wheat produces a harvest field (John 12:24-25), so Christ's death will produce abundant life for us now and in eternity.

2

The Fear of Death

A legend tells of a merchant in Baghdad who one day sent his servant to the market. Before long the servant came back, white and trembling, and in great agitation said to his master: "Down in the marketplace I was jostled by a woman in the crowd, and when I turned around I saw it was Death that jostled me. She looked at me and made a threatening gesture. Master, please lend me your horse, for I must hasten away to avoid her. I will ride to Samarra and there I will hide, and Death will not find me."

The merchant lent him his horse and the servant galloped away in great haste. Later the merchant went to the marketplace and saw Death standing in the crowd. He went over to her and asked, "Why did you frighten my servant this morning? Why did you make a threatening gesture?"

"That was not a threatening gesture," Death said. "It was only a start of surprise. I was astonished to see him in Baghdad, for I have an appointment with him tonight in Samarra."[3]

Each of us has an appointment in Samarra. But this doesn't need to be a cause of fear if we have put our trust in God, who alone holds the keys of life and death.

Death and the fear of it are described in the Bible. Hebrews 2:5-18 and its associated biblical themes can help us address several key questions: What is the fear of death and why do people have it? How have people sought to manage this fear? How is Satan related to this fear of death? How has the

Lord Jesus Christ conquered the fear of death?

What Is the Fear of Death?

Some people fear that by dying they will cease to exist. It is impossible to imagine what this would be like, since thinking assumes being. It is painful, however, to imagine life going on in our families or societies without us, as though we had vanished and become nonpersons. This idea of personal annihilation was not widely considered as man's destiny until the modern era. It is contrary to Scripture, which teaches that our personal identities continue after physical death.

A more common fear is that existence after death is so radically different from this life that preparing for or adjusting to it will be impossible. This is the fear of the unknown, the fear of the dying process, the fear of losing a familiar, supportive environment. This idea affects everyone to some degree, but should not haunt any of us. Clear biblical teaching and supportive relationships can lessen our uncertainty and help us face this major life change.

Why Are People Afraid of Death?

Though fear of death usually falls into one of the two aforementioned categories, other factors can amplify those feelings.

In the ancient world, many people were familiar with physical death but had intense cultural obsessions with it. Ancient citizens often inflicted physical punishments on themselves in an effort to satisfy evil gods and prevent demon-inflicted death.[4] This terror of blood-hungry spirits sometimes motivated people to practice human sacrifice as appeasement. The friends and family of a deceased person also thought they needed magic rituals to keep the dead person's ghost from returning to do harm. The need for protection from evil spirits characterized the ancient worldview.

In contrast, the God of Abraham deserved but did not demand the most precious gift of human life (Gen. 22:1-19). In fact, Abraham's near sacrifice of Isaac dramatically illustrates God's desire to provide an alternative. God ultimately provided a substitute sacrifice for the whole human race by providing

Jesus Christ as the Lamb of God (John 1:29).

In the modern world, many people are unfamiliar with physical death and are obsessed with preserving life. Since the advent of modern medicine, there have been fewer epidemics and early deaths. When death does occur today, it is usually isolated in the mechanized and institutional world of hospitals. This creates a new fear—the fear of being deserted in a lonely hospital room when you are dying. Because few of us die at home, most family members are unfamiliar with the dying process. When people die within sight of others, it is usually because that death resulted from crime, war, or accident. The modern citizen also faces the possibility of "megadeath" through nuclear holocaust. All these factors give death an especially cruel, unwelcome image today.

Common Responses to the Fear of Death

There seem to be three common ways in which people seek to dilute their anxieties about death. Some choose *hedonism*. They seek to selfishly indulge in pleasure before death snatches the opportunity away. The ancient slogan of this lifestyle was, "Eat, drink, and be merry, for tomorrow we die." The modern version says, "You only go around once in life, so grab for all the gusto you can." The strategy seems to be, "Ignore life after death; numb yourself to the fear of physical death by total self-gratification now."

Others choose *pessimism*. Since death is coming and is dreaded, nothing matters. Life is worthless and painful, so you might as well get the dying over with. Living this way is like trying to enjoy reading a magazine in the dentist's waiting room while the sound of dental surgery sends shivers up your spine. As Byron said, "Those whom the gods love, die young."

The third way people seek to minimize their fear of death is through *denial*—avoiding all thought of it. They devote their efforts to death opposites—health, strength, fame, offspring, wealth, etc. Some religious and philosophical systems actually try to distract people from ever facing the reality of human aging and individual death. The Italian Renaissance artist Dante, for example, felt that romantic love could keep one from dwelling uncomfortably on death. With this goal in mind, he painted Paolo and Francesca locked in an eternal, anguished embrace in the Inferno.

Satan and the Fear of Death

According to Hebrews 2:14-15, Satan uses his power to enslave people. Furthermore, his ability to manipulate and exaggerate their latent fear of death often makes people vulnerable to his deceptions.

It is apparent from Job 1:12 that Satan does not innately have the power to kill. But he does seek to produce sinful behavior in people, in opposition to God. When one rebels against God, one risks inviting the consequence of sin, which is death (Rom. 6:23; James 1:13-15). Though death has spiritual, physical, and eternal aspects, all death is ultimately the result of sin. To the degree that Satan can incite people to sin, he can influence the divine consequences of sin—death.

Satan plays a mind game. He wants to seduce angry people to murder. He wants to tempt discouraged people to commit suicide. He wants to capture people who are uneasy about death and elevate their intimidation to the level of morbid terror and immobilizing anxiety. But God wants to give us freedom from the fear of death. The Lord thus attacks the source of this fear through the person and work of Jesus Christ.

How Has Jesus Conquered the Fear of Death?

According to the Epistle to the Hebrews, Jesus is superior to angels, to Moses, and to the Old Testament high priest. But even though He is superior, He has taken an interest in inferior man (2:5-8). His interest in man is so great that He has humbly experienced death in human form for mankind (2:9). This temporary reduction in rank has united Him with flesh-and-blood humanity in a way that allows Him to call human beings "brothers" (2:10-13). Since He has identified with man in his mortal weakness (2:10, 14), He can be an effective priest (2:16-18). Since He has been exalted above man's weaknesses, He can receive glory and make effective satisfaction for sin (2:9, 11, 14-17; Phil. 2:9; Rom. 8:17).

Jesus took on the role of man so that He could engage

mankind's archenemy, Satan (2:14). Having won that battle, Christ can rescue those whom Satan has manipulated through the fear of death. Jesus offers liberation to a life without this shackling fear.

Life in the Factory: An Analogy

Consider an illustration. Imagine that you're a poor factory worker during the Great Depression. You know that your job is your only lifeline to survival. You live in fear that your supervisor might fire you. You know that if you lose this job, there will be no replacement; starvation might be your fate. You'll do anything to keep this job—work sick, work overtime. You are totally vulnerable to the whims of your supervisor.

Suppose that one day a high-level inspector comes to your factory. He is dressed as a common laborer so that he can work beside you and get an accurate view of your working conditions and the illegitimate influence of the factory supervisor. Once he has seen enough of the harassment, he fires the supervisor and installs himself as the new man in charge.

It is like this in the spiritual realm. Many people have been laboring for centuries in a spiritually dark workhouse. They have lived in spiritual poverty, afraid of the manipulative tyrant who seems capable of taking their very lives. This supervisor can't actually kill the poor workers because the law stops him short of that, but his influence seems nearly that deadly. The workers live on the very edge of death, and intimidation by the supervisor constantly brings the fear of death to their minds.

Our Lord Jesus, aware of the corruption in this "factory," stepped onto the production line with His overalls and hard hat. He sweated, worked, and was threatened so that He could understand the plight of the workers. Once His credibility as a worker had been tested and His superiority to the adversary proven, Jesus "fired" him. Though that old supervisor still exists, his power to harass the workers is gone. He may stand at the gate, shouting intimidations at the workers as they enter the factory, but they need not pay any attention to him. His authority has been taken away. In fact, he faces criminal charges and is just awaiting deportation.

Christ has overpowered and disarmed Satan (Luke 11:14-

22). Christ's appearance among humanity has destroyed the works of the devil (1 John 3:8). It is just a short while before Satan receives his full and final punishment (Rom. 16:20; Rev. 20:10, 14).

No More Sting

Though it is not biblically correct to say that death is gone, we can say that the fear of death is conquered in Jesus Christ (2 Tim. 1:10; 1 Cor. 15:26, 54-57). Just as we might still be intimidated by the sight of a snake which has been milked of venom,[5] however, there is still the potential for some residual fear.

One elderly saint, dying at home with cancer, became somewhat fearful. She wasn't afraid of being dead; she knew she would be with her Saviour in a place without sorrow, darkness, or tears. But she was a little fearful of the dying process. After all, she had obviously never been through it before, though she had survived cancer twice. Her main worry was that she would be alone when she died, with no companion in the room. She thought she would want to talk with or touch someone in her final moments, as we all probably would.

This fear of being alone was removed by the teamwork of her family and friends. Then it was revealed that she also feared people would lose patience as they waited for her to die, that she would be a bother to those who cared for her. This fear was dispelled as family and friends reaffirmed their love for her and their respect for her dignity. This was *her* disease in *her* body in *her* house, she was reminded, and she had every right to go at her own pace. With these assurances she was able to rest again.

As Christians, we need not be terrorized by death. It is true that we will never enjoy death or anticipate the dying process as a happy one. But we can live life fully, even in the light of terminal illness and imminent death. Numerous believers have been able to face death with acceptance and genuine faith. Though they don't *want* to die, they are not *afraid* to die.

There is sadness in loss, but also anticipation of relief and reunion in heaven. As God's children we will be changed (Rom. 8:15, 21, 35-39). We don't know what all the changes will involve, but we will become like Christ in some ways (1 John

3:1-3). We can focus on this element of hope and be motivated to live purer lives as well.

A Dark Cave?

Our greatest comfort concerning death comes in knowing that Jesus Christ has experienced death already—and will be with us when we die. This truth reminds me how, as a child, I was invited to enter a dark cave for the first time. After I had stepped into the cave's mouth, I retreated for fear. A braver companion went in, disappearing into the dark—and soon exited the cave from another point on the hill.

After seeing his successful experience and hearing his assurance to go with me, I held his hand and entered the unknown. Soon I too stepped from the intimidating darkness into the light on the other side of the hill. Blinking and stretching, I left behind me the fear I had felt about the cave.

So it is with the Christian and death. Each of us faces an unknown "cave" that can frighten us. But Christ has already successfully navigated the cave of death and emerged in the sunlight of resurrection. We may shrink at first from the unknown, but can have ultimate confidence that Christ has gone before us—and will accompany us through death into the light of eternity.

3

The Death Movement and the Word of God

An ancient parable tells the story of a mother whose son died without warning. She could not believe that her only child was dead. *Certainly he must only be ill*, she thought. Desperate, she sought a medicine that could heal her son. As she searched, people mocked her for her foolishness.

Eventually the woman found a wise man who told her to go from house to house in every village and ask whether death had ever come there. If she found a home where death had never come, she was to get some grains of mustard seed from this family and bring them to the wise man, who could make a medicine for the woman's son.

The woman did as she was told—but could not find a family in which death had not occurred. She found that death had touched every family and every individual in some way. As she shared her grief and grieved with others, she was able to accept the reality of her son's death. She was not able to reverse her son's death, but could heal her own denial of death and bury the son.

Like that woman, many of us—along with our whole culture—try to deny death. This is not surprising when we consider our unique time in history. Modern medicine has greatly increased the average life span, and has given us the hospital and nursing home to shield us from the most acute examples of aging, illness, and death. An alarming increase in secular thinking has also caused more and more people to reject the biblical notion of afterlife. The old motto, "Prepare to meet your Maker," meets with laughter and skepticism.

Such challenges to biblical thinking are dangers to the naive but opportunities to the wise. To be spiritually wise we should assess modern attitudes toward death and know how to respond to them.

Death: The Secular and Psychic Perspectives

After decades of denying mortality, many people have begun to show renewed interest in death. As a Christian sociologist has observed, "Studies on death, dying, bereavement, and related topics flooded the market in the 1970s. The subject is no longer a taboo topic. . . . It is becoming institutionalized as a solidly established area for study, research, and professional training."[6]

With the large post-World-War-I-baby-boom generation now entering older age, and their children, the post-World-War-II-baby-boom group becoming middle-aged providers for their parents, it's no wonder people are asking questions about death that haven't been asked for decades. But now the questions seem to come with a highly secular bias or from a psychic viewpoint. In either case, the biblical idea that death is a natural process under God's control and transitional to afterlife is discarded as being too meager for 20th-century thinkers.

The new "death and dying" movement, also called thanatology (the study of death), seems to be plagued by two extremes. On one hand are rigid scientific types who focus on prolonging and analyzing biological life; on the other are nearly occult psychic advocates.

Not long ago I visited Sarah, a woman with terminal bone cancer. Over a period of weeks I also met her physician, who was perfectly cast in the secularist mold. Sarah was a sincere Christian and had accepted her terminal diagnosis, but her doctor had no such belief and was fighting the cancer like a frenzied warrior. Convinced that there was no life beyond the grave, he felt her earthly life must be preserved at all costs. At his insistence she went through rigorous treatments which resulted in the loss of her hair, much of her body weight, and her hope for a cure.

Sarah and her sisters came to accept her imminent death as

God's will. They were able to laugh and cry together, to share precious memories. But Sarah's doctor, who dealt with cancer patients all the time, could not see the bigger view of life as emotional, spiritual, eternal. He was obsessed with the statistical probabilities, the prognosis, and her physical death. When she witnessed to him about her faith, he became angry that she had "given up." He wanted to do heroic surgery to try to "save" her life, but she didn't want it, didn't need it, and couldn't survive it. She was content with the knowledge that she would die soon. "When the pain gets real bad at night and I am alone," Sarah would tell her doctor, "that's when I sing and hear the angels singing with me." This kind of talk would drive the doctor back to his coping strategy—heroic medical intervention to save the physical body.

Finally Sarah and her family and I told the doctor that no more surgery would be permitted. Enraged, he said, "You people are standing outside a burning house, and you know there is somebody inside who needs to be rescued. But you refuse to help. That's almost like murder or suicide or something." With that final accusation, he withdrew from Sarah and never visited her again while she was awake. She died two weeks later, as she had hoped she would, on Easter morning.

Sarah's doctor knew a lot about death. But his knowledge was only biological, too rigidly scientific. All he could see was the body, because he was blind to the spirit.

While Sarah's doctor focused on her body at the exclusion of her soul, psychics ignore the body in search of the soul. The psychic influence in the death and dying movement is mainly an overreaction to earlier denial of death and to current secularism. People who can't deny death any longer, and who feel the secularism of our times is empty, have rebounded to a new religion. After comparing spiritualist themes in Hinduism and studying near-death and "out-of-body" experiences, the psychics are convinced they understand death.

Dr. Raymond Moody, Jr., author of the controversial book *Life after Life* (Stackpole Books), talked to many people who claimed that they came close to dying or were resuscitated from death. These people, according to Moody, have recollections of existing psychically or spiritually while they were "dead." He reports that they often felt enhanced, saw their own bodies, heard a buzzing sound, and traveled through a tunnel. Sometimes they also described meeting friends and encountering a "being of light" before they returned to their bodies. Perhaps most important are the beliefs that grow out of these experiences. Moody cites this testimony: "Life is like imprisonment. In this state, we just can't understand what prisons these bodies are. Death is such a release—like an escape from prison. That's the best thing I can think of to compare it to."[7]

Tragically, the false teachings of this psychic extreme can be found even in children's books and the magazines available at the supermarket.[8] Some of the most dangerous ideas proposed by the psychic thanatologists are as follows:

- Near-death and out-of-body experiences are the truest revelations of afterlife.
- Biblical teachings on heaven and hell are incorrect.
- There is no judgment after death.
- The disembodied person becomes all-knowing in death.
- The body is of little value and will not be resurrected.
- People will be reincarnated.
- The living can communicate with the dead.
- The human mind is capable of supernatural feats such as remembering former lives and receiving messages from spirit guides.
- Eastern religions provide the most accurate teachings on afterlife.

The believer must remember that the Bible is true and without error. It forbids any attempt at occult communication with the dead (Deut. 18:10-12; 1 Chron. 10:13-14) and warns against apostate demonic doctrines (1 Tim. 4:1-3). Furthermore, the Bible affirms the judgment of God, the centrality of Christ, the deceptiveness of Satan, and the resurrection of the body.

A Balanced Perspective

The modern death and dying movement commits major errors when it excludes biblical teaching and moves to the secularist or psychic extreme. Scripture teaches a balance between body, soul, and spirit (1 Thes. 5:23). The Creator has made life and death to permeate our whole beings—physically, emotionally, and spiritually. Furthermore, He superintends the dynamics of life, death, and the afterlife.

It's encouraging to see how many Christians have a balanced perspective on death. They have committed themselves to caring for people who are sick, aged, dying, or bereaved. They have seen the Bible's emphasis on caring for people in need and have not run from these painful realities.

Many Christians have shown their avoidance of the secularist and psychic extremes by entering the health care and education professions, as well as church ministries, for the sake of Christ. Pastors with spiritual balance have also become leaders in the hospice movement, helping care for people who choose to die at home. Whole churches have become known for their lay care-giving teams and sensitive death education.

A Biblical Perspective

There is at least one similarity between the Bible and the death and dying movement, however. Both emphasize the need for a realistic attitude about death.

The Bible views death as the normal finish line for every runner in the race of life. Death is the most predictable developmental stage, the ultimate life-change event. When Joshua was dying (Josh. 23:1-2), he summoned national leaders so that he could announce his coming death. He said, "Now behold, today I am going the way of all the earth" (23:14). He did not seem to feel bitter disillusionment and fear because his death was imminent. Instead he saw himself as moving into the final phase of a normal cycle that characterizes the whole universe. He was not "going to meet the grim reaper." He was "going the way of all the earth." He, like all organic things, was moving predictably through the life-death sequence according to the design of the Creator.[9]

Such acceptance of death is also evidenced in King David's final scene. "As David's time to die drew near, he charged Solomon his son, saying, 'I am going the way of all the earth' " (1 Kings 2:1-2).

Joshua and David affirmed the normalcy of death. They moved toward it with a tolerant worldview and positive communication with their bystanding survivors. They saw themselves not as dehumanized cellular machines but as personal beings animated by God Himself (Ps. 104:29-30).

Even though the Bible portrays death as predictable, it also acknowledges the feelings of pain and loss which surround death. Changes are always upsetting; we are creatures who value stability, familiarity, and routine. Since death is the ultimate change, it is bound to upset or disorient even the strongest of us. Every change creates stress, demands energy for us to make needed adjustments, and takes creativity and faith for us to view it in a healthy way.

If you think back over your life, you can recall many significant changes. They include most of the following: your birth, the births of others in your family, starting school, moving, puberty, gaining and losing friendships, acquiring and losing valued possessions, moving out of your parents' home, gaining and losing jobs, marrying, realizing the achievement or failure of certain dreams, retirement, etc. Each change had the potential of producing growth in your life and family. Each change or crisis had the potential of crystallizing your identity (answering the question, "Who am I?") and focusing your direction (answering the question, "What am I living for?"). Thus we have all experienced many little "births" and "deaths" throughout life. Adjusting to our "little deaths" and to our ultimate death places stress on us, but also offers opportunities for personal growth.

People who haven't adjusted to life's losses commonly have problems with living. They often deny realities, live in the past, don't say what they really mean, or close themselves off from others. But those who have learned to adjust usually are more realistic about life, cope better with the present, are more genuine in expressing their feelings, and are open to change and growth. They are cut from the same cloth as Joshua and David. When we adopt a biblical view of life and a balanced perspective on death, we can make the mercy of God believable to those who suffer (2 Cor. 1:3-4). Our inner hope will be obvious to doubters (1 Peter 3:15), and Jesus Christ will be lifted up to all men (Col. 1:18).

4

Good Grief

Charles Schulz's lovable cartoon character Charlie Brown personifies our most sincere failures. His instinctive response to each unfortunate turn of events is, "Good Grief!"

Good grief? It sounds contradictory. Could grief ever be a good thing?

Grief is a God-given emotion, a coping mechanism invented by the Creator. In that sense, grief is good. The circumstances which bring us grief may be difficult to handle. But our capacity to grieve is a healthy trait—one to be understood, not regretted. When we go through a loss or major adjustment, grief may be the most therapeutic response we can make.

The Bible refers to grief hundreds of times. From these references we can learn that grief is a normal human reaction to loss; that grief can express itself in many ways; and that grief is understood by God. In a society that often sees expressions of grief as signs of weakness or spiritual immaturity, we especially can profit from a look at Scripture's teaching on the subject.

Grief: a Normal Human Reaction

It's comforting to know that the Bible treats grief as a normal response to loss. With great sensitivity and insight, God's Word describes several facets of this human reaction:

1. *Grief helps us express the value someone or something holds for us.* When Jacob died, his son Joseph wept and kissed

him (Gen. 50:1). His grief helped him express his great affection for his father. This was not a sign of weakness or fear, but of emotional strength. When Jesus' friend Lazarus died, our Lord—the perfect Man—wept (John 11:35-36, 38). In fact, He wept so openly and fully that bystanders remarked, "Behold how He loved him!" (v. 36)

Because grief normally connotes value, God forbade some Old Testament prophets to weep for pagans or apostate Israelites. Ezekiel and Jeremiah were not to weep for those who were punished by God (Jer. 16:5-7; Ezek. 24:15-24). Had they publicly grieved for these people, it would have implied affection for those of whom God had disapproved.

2. *Grief can be expressed through music or Scripture readings.* Sometimes our feelings run so deeply that we cannot put words to them. Established lyrics often allow us to ventilate these emotions. David found that music was his main grief outlet when he sang laments over Saul and Abner (2 Sam. 1:17-27; 3:33-34). Jeremiah also used songs to express his grief over Josiah's death (2 Chron. 35:25). When the nation of Israel suffered its destruction under Babylon, poets sang songs of lament (Jer. 9:10-11; Lam. 1–5).

3. *Grief may last for an extended period.* It is unrealistic to expect grief over a significant loss to pass quickly. When Aaron died, the nation mourned for thirty days (Num. 20:29). When Jacob died, the nation of Egypt mourned seventy days (Gen. 50:1-3); afterward Jacob's immediate family mourned for another seven days (Gen. 50:10).

Grief may not be resolved by the passing of a difficult day or a trying conversation. Familiar objects, places, birthdays, or anniversaries may also give new life to old feelings.

I've seen how deeply and how long grief can be felt. I was asked to come quickly when one man had been rushed to the hospital; when I arrived, the family was gathered around a bed in the intensive care unit, surrounded by life-support machines. A middle-age man had suffered a heart attack, and there was grave doubt that he would survive; his heart was beating ever so slowly and his lungs had cancer.

As we stood around the bed, there was great pain in each relative's face and voice. The patient was unconscious, apparently dying, so family members were asked to say their goodbyes. With great grief they whispered their affection and touched their loved one, then left the room.

The dying man's brother, however, couldn't bring himself to go. He refused to leave in case his brother needed him. There he stood, tears flowing, talking to his brother and rubbing his arm to stimulate him—to keep him alive. The two of us stayed at the bedside for another hour, when the heart monitor suddenly showed no more life. The heart had stopped; the man had died.

Again the brother was asked to leave so the hospital staff could disconnect the respirator and care for the body. But his grief still wouldn't let him go. He stayed and watched, finally becoming convinced that his brother was dead. He and I talked and prayed. We found the other relatives, and many of them cried; grief was carried powerfully for weeks by each member of the family. Even months after the death, just a mention of the deceased's name or of that night in the hospital would bring speechless tears to his brother. That was normal. He loved his brother and would miss him.

4. *Grief may make it difficult to resume life's routines.* After a major loss, it may seem hard to resume normal activities. David found that after Abner had died, he couldn't bring himself to eat (2 Sam. 3:35). Later when Absalom died, David even regretted being alive (2 Sam. 18:33). He could hardly imagine going on without his son. The grief of these multiple losses taxed his nervous system more than he felt he could bear.

The Bible also records the final days of the elderly priest Eli (1 Sam. 4:12-18). Eli felt the shock of loss when he received word from the battlefield that the army had been defeated, the ark had been taken, and his two sons were dead. Immediately Eli fell backward, broke his neck, and died. Later when his daughter-in-law heard the same bad news, she went into premature labor and died (1 Sam. 4:19-22).

When we go through losses, it may be difficult at first to resume life's normal routine. Bereavement may even increase our susceptibility to sickness or death. But grief can be resolved as we remember more realistically the object or person lost. As we assess the loss with growing realism and continue to interact socially, we share the work of grief. This healing process allows us to reinvest in life even though life has changed for us.

The Stages of Grief

No two people will handle the same loss in the same way. Circumstances are different, and so are people. In fact, even one person going through similar losses at two different times in his life may handle them quite differently. But most people pass through at least some of the following grief phases:

Major Types of Grief Response	
Before a Loss	Preparatory Grief
After a Loss	Denial Anger Bargaining Depression Acceptance

1. *Preparatory grief.* When we receive news of an upcoming loss, we may begin the grieving process.[10] Hezekiah the king wept when he was told that he would die of a fatal illness (Isa. 38:1-3). Apparently Hezekiah hadn't even felt sick. But the prophet gave him the difficult news much as a doctor could give us a terminal diagnosis before we felt the effects of a disease. Jesus also grieved in anticipation when His arrest was imminent (Matt. 26:37-38; Heb. 5:7).

2. *Progressive grief.* As health care experts have found, grief can express itself through a series of stages or states.[11] Our first reaction to a loss may be *denial* or shock. We just can't believe the tragedy has happened to us; we are numb emotionally or reject the idea as a bad dream or a lie.

When Jesus told His disciples that He would die soon, Peter was unable to grasp the idea (Mark 8:31-33). Peter was spiritually and emotionally unable to believe that Jesus would soon be gone. In fact, Peter rebuked Jesus for bringing up the idea.

Sharon was one person who went through the denial phase. The mother of a college student, she would proudly tell others how her daughter was studying nursing at the university. Then everything went wrong for her daughter; a simple infection turned into a fever, and within forty-eight hours the daughter was in a coma.

"Why are the doctors talking about brain damage?" Sharon asked. "Why are they hinting at death? I just prayed for healing, and God told me our daughter is going to live. I don't want any doctors or visitors talking about death! I have faith in God, not medicine." Sharon was denying the diagnosis; she couldn't accept what appeared to be certain death. Anger at the doctors and wishing for a miracle were Sharon's only messages for two days as the girl lingered between life and death. But anger and wishing didn't work, and the young nursing student died.

Sharon was numb. She felt as if she were in a dream. She would wake up at night because she imagined she heard her daughter pulling into the driveway. She considered quitting her job, taking her daughter's textbooks, and going to nursing school herself. "It was such a great goal—why should it go to waste?" she asked.

With help from others, Sharon realized that in a sense she was trying to *become* her daughter to keep the nursing dream alive. But the nursing dream had died with her daughter. So Sharon grieved again as she saw that she had not only lost her only child—she had also lost the fulfillment of watching her daughter achieve. To heal from this loss would require Sharon to find other ways to be fulfilled, and new goals other than reliving her daughter's life. As she grew beyond denial, she was able to begin healing.

Once we have let the fact of our loss touch us closely, our grief may express itself as *anger*. Rage may seem to leap out of us against God, a doctor, or family members.

Mary and Martha must have felt such anger after they had sent for Jesus to come and heal Lazarus (John 11:3, 21, 32). Jesus didn't hurry (11:6), and by the time He arrived, Lazarus had died. One of the sisters responded to Jesus, "If You had been here, my brother would not have died" (John 11:21, 32). These words imply belief that Jesus could have healed. But they also contain an element of confusion and anger over the fact that Jesus didn't help when He could have. Job also felt this twinge of anger when he shouted to God, "Thou hast made me as clay; and wouldst Thou turn me into dust again?" (Job 10:9)

Our grief may next leave us feeling like *bargaining* with God or with people to diminish or distance our loss. Hezekiah bargained with the Lord to get a fifteen-year extension on his life (2 Kings 20:1-7; Isa. 38:1-21). The psalmist also begged, wept, and prayed that the Lord would protect him from his own imminent death (Ps. 88). Even Jesus prayed to the Father that if redemption could be achieved in any way short of execution, this was His request (Matt. 26:39, 42, 44). Yet Christ had the maturity and insight to offer to undergo any circumstance, no matter how painful, if it was the Father's will.

Prayer in these instances is a form of bargaining. It is a candid expression of feelings to a God who cares. The one praying is not trying to persuade a reluctant deity to do something contrary to His nature; rather prayer clarifies our desires in a matter.

Believers who are doubting or struggling with a problem often need to pray the most. To talk openly with the Lord is to follow the example of great biblical characters who bargained with God. They were convinced that He cared about their feelings, thoughts, and circumstances. We must remember, though, that mature prayer also requires willingness to allow God to readjust our thinking to His.

Another stage of grief through which people go is *depression*. Once we see that our loss cannot be reduced by bargaining, we may go through a period of lethargy or seeming lifelessness. While David's child was dying, he was unable to eat, drink, sleep, or converse (2 Sam. 12:16-18). He prayed and fasted. We may go through a similar period of depression; once this depression lifts, we can begin to reinvest in life.

The final stage of grief is *acceptance,* or genuine grief. In this phase, one fully acknowledges the loss and gets beyond attempts to ignore feelings (denial) or dispose of feelings (anger, bargaining, depression).

We can come to the place where we truly grieve, as Jesus did for His friend Lazarus (John 11:35-36, 38). Joseph also came to that place at the death of his father (Gen. 50:1, 10). After the Apostle Paul had been thrown in prison, he came to recognize that God was in control of his loss of freedom and potential loss of life (Phil. 1:12, 21-24, 29-30). He said, "I have learned to be content" in favorable or poor circumstances (Phil. 4:11-13). He had moved beyond his sense of personal loss to see God's control.

The expression of grief in progressive stages is more than an emotional outlet. It is the common process of healing and growth.

Grief: Understood by God

The Bible comforts us with the knowledge that God is open and sympathetic to our grief. We know He understands our grief because Scripture describes Him as capable of grieving, as drawn to those who grieve, and as interested in solving grief-producing problems.

When the human race had become so spiritually bankrupt that no one but Noah paid attention to God, Scripture says God was grieved (Gen. 6:6). He had lost that most important relationship to His creatures, one in which they were responsive and obedient. As already mentioned, when the Son of God experienced the loss of His friend Lazarus, He grieved (John 11:35-36, 38). Paul writes that when believers fail to respond to the promptings of the Holy Spirit, the Spirit is grieved (Eph. 4:30). God understands grief through personal experience.

The Gospels depict Jesus as drawn to people in pain and crisis. When our Lord was on earth, He spent much of His time serving people who were in pain and crisis. In Mark's short Gospel, we observe Jesus being drawn to the paralyzed youth (2:1-12), the diseased woman (5:25-34), the synagogue officer's daughter (5:35-43), the Syrian woman's daughter (7:24-30), the demon-possessed boy (9:14-27), and the blind man (10:46-52). This Gospel is typical of the others. It shows that Jesus is inclined to be near people who are in need.

The Epistles further portray Jesus as a caring, sympathetic High Priest. A look at the Epistle to the Hebrews reveals that our Lord had a human body with all the physical limitations of our own (2:17-18). He can therefore sympathize with our weaknesses (4:15-16). Because He identifies with us, we are encouraged to draw near Him with confidence. Through His own sufferings He became perfectly qualified to be our High

Priest (5:7-10). Thus He can understand our grief as well as overcome our problems.

We also know that God must understand our pain because He intends to overcome the problems which cause us grief. This is why Isaiah speaks of a time when death, calamity, and violence will be ended (Isa. 65:17-25). The Apostle John predicts an end to fear, sorrow, and death (Rev. 21:4). And Paul comforts the Thessalonian church with the hope of Christ's return (1 Thes. 4:16-18).

The Power of Hope

Hope in God's empathy, purpose, and goodness can turn our tragedies into testimonies. One woman, Elaine, had the opportunity to discover this when her phone rang one afternoon and an unfamiliar voice spoke: "Elaine, you don't know me—but I am the physician at County Construction, your husband's company. We've had an accident this morning involving your husband. I'd like you to come down to the hospital right away if you can. I've just called a taxi for you, which should be arriving any minute. If you have a friend or neighbor nearby who could come with you, I'd bring him or her along."

Elaine was in shock. Within minutes she was in the taxi, destined to find out that a heavy machine had fallen and crushed her engineer husband. *How could this make any sense?* she thought. She had two teenage boys who desperately needed a father, and now he was gone.

In the weeks that followed, Elaine's thoughts would swing back and forth from panic to hope. Sometimes she was in such agony for herself and the boys that she thought she'd die from the pain. At other times familiar words from the Bible would challenge her: "All things work together for good to them that love God" (Rom. 8:28, KJV). As the months passed, she became aware of changes in the people around her. Some friends and church members would avoid her, not knowing what to say. Others offered trite answers that ignored her grief. Some lumped her in with the young singles and divorcees.

But there were a few who listened lovingly to Elaine for hours at any time of the day or night. They heard her shock, her angry complaints. They sought her out when she withdrew from them. They gave her spiritual and human comfort as Christ would have, helping her begin to find purpose and meaning in this tragedy.

Today, as Elaine looks back at her pain, she and her friends can point to some good that came from her loss. One of her sons, confronted with the Gospel at his father's funeral, gave his life to Christ. Elaine herself has become an unusually gifted servant who cares for people in trouble. Because of her faith and the faithfulness of God and some of His people, a son's life and a mother's ministry have become testimonies of healing.

It is encouraging to know that grief is a normal, healthy response to loss, and that God understands, cares, and wants to bring us through grief to healing. Because He cares about us, we can be candid with Him about our grief. And because He will one day put an end to many forms of suffering, we can rejoice and comfort each other with hope.

PART TWO
SUFFERING

5

The Suffering
of Jesus

There stood the young clergyman, trying to give comfort to the parents whose son had just been killed in a car accident. "Just remember that Jesus has nothing, nothing, *nothing* whatever to do with this accident," he said. "This just happened. It all boils down to chances and choices. We all make choices to drive and take chances with drunk drivers in the other lane. Just remember that Jesus has nothing to do with this accident."

The intentions of this man were notable in that he was trying to relieve the family of a burden. He wanted to say that this accident was not the result of a morbid and purposeless punishment by God. But he left the impression that random chance rules everything—that God is not in control. It was crucial for those sufferers to eventually hear that "Jesus has everything, everything, *everything* to do with helping you cope with this accident and helping you discover purpose and growth through this loss." Jesus identifies with sufferers, seeks spiritual companionship with them, and offers them grace to grow and find meaning in their pain.

When Christ became a Man and lived on earth, He was guaranteed pain. He lived among us that He might be one of us, understanding our suffering and weakness (Heb. 2:1-15). The fact that He voluntarily suffered and died for us assures that He has everything to do with our suffering. He identifies with us and seeks to give us hope.

No one else in history suffered more—or more unjustly—

45

than Jesus Christ did. And no one cares more about our pain than He does.

The Unjust Trials

While Jesus was predicting to His unbelieving followers that He would die by crucifixion, the religious leaders were plotting a kidnap and murder scheme against Him. Ironically, the divine plan and the human scheme seemed to develop side by side. Soon our Lord was anointed in advance for burial (v. 12) and betrayed by His own disciple (vv. 15, 25). He predicted bloodshed (v. 28) and confusion among His sheep (v. 31).

While Jesus and His drowsy followers awaited the events of that evening in the Garden of Gethsemane, armed temple soldiers were marching to His arrest (v. 47). The cowardice of the soldiers in arresting Him under cover of night was matched only by the fearful retreat of His own disciples.

Soon Jesus stood alone in a private interrogation session before the high priest Caiaphas (v. 57). After this brief and biased pretrial hearing, the judges marched Jesus before the seventy-member Sanhedrin. In the larger Sanhedrin trial, Jesus was quickly condemned of blasphemy by two false witnesses (vv. 59-66). He had been overheard declaring His ability to destroy and rebuild the temple in only three days. Since the religious leaders did not believe that Jesus was the Messiah, His claim of authority and power to do the miraculous (i.e., rebuilding the literal Jerusalem temple or even raising His body from death) was considered blasphemy.

Once the Sanhedrin members were persuaded that Jesus was a blaspheming, false Messiah, they began a torrent of humiliation. They tore their clothes as a self-righteous sign that they were in the presence of a heretic; they spit on Him; they blindfolded Him and beat Him. Taunting, they asked Him to tell who was beating Him despite the blindfold, but He chose not to play their game. For several hours He continued to be verbally and physically abused.

Since nighttime interrogation and trial were illegal according to Jewish law, the Sanhedrin dismissed and reconvened at dawn. But there was another problem: Blasphemy was a capital offense according to Jewish law, and the occupying Romans had taken away the privilege of local rulers to try capital cases. This meant the Sanhedrin would have to come up with a civil crime of which to accuse Jesus if He was to be executed under Roman law.[12] Blasphemy was not a Roman crime; if anything, it was a Roman sport.

After a brief strategy session at dawn, the Sanhedrin went through the formality of charging Jesus with blasphemy worthy of death (Matt. 27:1-2). Jesus was then transferred as a prisoner under guard to the local Roman governor, Pontius Pilate. It was in this civil hearing that Jewish accusers sought to prove Jesus worthy of Roman crucifixion. As the session labored on, Pilate heard accusations that Jesus had tried to mislead the nation (sedition), to forbid paying taxes (insubordination), and to be the self-proclaimed "King of the Jews" (high treason). Though Jesus accepted this final accusation (Matt. 27:11), Pilate was unwilling to condemn Him to death. Pilate felt caught between the fate of Jesus, a religious troublemaker, and the Sanhedrin, a persuaded religious court.

Pilate decided to defer this unmanageable trial to the governor of Galilee, Herod Antipas. Perhaps by submitting to Antipas' authority, Pilate could rectify the long-standing bitterness between Antipas and himself.

As the morning dragged on, Christ found Himself before Herod Antipas. This was to be but another mockery of justice. Antipas, at first fearful that Jesus was the decapitated John the Baptist, sought a display of miraculous power; Christ refused to honor his request. Christ was then dressed in a purple robe and His claim to be King was derided. When the cruel entertainment was finished, Antipas sent Christ back to Pilate under military guard.

Faced with a dilemma, Pilate offered the crowd two candidates for release—Barabbas and Jesus. The Jewish leaders convinced the crowd that Jesus was a blasphemer and should die. When Pilate hesitated for one last moment, the conspirators implied that he would be viewed as disloyal to Caesar if he released Jesus (John 19:12). How could Pilate release a self-proclaimed "King of the Jews" and not express disloyalty to the Caesar in Rome who was the "King of the World"?

The decision was made: Jesus would be crucified. In a weak act of symbolism, Pilate washed his hands as though claiming innocence in the execution. Ignorantly the crowds chanted that they would take full responsibility for His death. For them this had become an act of orthodoxy; they would self-righteously kill the blaspheming false Messiah.

Christ's Losses

Many people who reflect on the suffering of Christ focus solely on His physical death. That death was torturous. But our Lord suffered in many other ways on behalf of fallen mankind. Late in His life He lost the following:

1. The loyalty of Judas as that disciple betrayed Him;
2. The support of Peter, James, and John as He agonized in the Garden of Gethsemane;
3. The commitment of His twelve disciples as they doubted, feared, and retreated;
4. All genuine protection under the religious laws and leaders of Judaism;
5. All genuine protection under the civil laws and leaders of Rome;
6. His reputation, by being declared a criminal guilty of treason and blasphemy;
7. His physical and psychological safety through physical and verbal abuse;
8. His privacy as He was stripped and humiliated before His interrogators;
9. All right to legal representation;
10. The prospect of His spiritual mission being nationally understood;
11. His credibility—by His apparent inability to prophesy, work miracles, fight back against His aggressors, rescue Himself, or rule as a King; and
12. The support of the common folk in less than one week's time (compare the "Hosannas!" of the Triumphal Entry with the "Crucify Him!" of the angry crowds).

Christ was used to losses. Those he suffered late in life were in many cases extensions of earlier losses. He had already lost the following:

1. The right to remain in His eternal, glorious form outside the earthly dimension of sin, decay, and death;
2. The right to be born in proper surroundings;
3. The right to be born or raised in a significant city or tribal family;
4. The right to have a socially approved birth (since the virgin birth was interpreted to be an illegitimate one by many);
5. The support of His natural family;
6. The possibility of personal ease as He was frequently tired, hungry, thirsty, and poor;
7. Even the superficial loyalty which some people had given Him;
8. The feeling of physical safety, due to repeated murder attempts against Him;
9. The freedom to relax spiritually due to constant satanic and demonic opposition;
10. The tolerance of religious leaders when they began full-scale criticism against Him;
11. The confidence of His dearest friends, such as Mary and Martha, who criticized Him;
12. The loyalty of His key followers, as shown when Peter contradicted Him about His whole mission; and
13. The potential of having His work understood, such as when the healing of the blind man was challenged.

His Suffering and Death

In life and death, Christ was forsaken by all. Once He had been condemned to die by crucifixion, the death march began. Soldiers stripped Him of His mock robe and crown. They took from His hand the reed which had served as a "royal" scepter and repeatedly struck Him with it as He marched (Matt. 27:30). When His cross became too heavy to bear, a bystander was required to carry it to Golgotha.

When Christ arrived at the execution site, He was stripped naked and nailed to a low wooden cross. Though He had already been brutalized, He refused a stupefying drink. Pain shot through His body, caused by the tense position, nails, and cuts. He experienced thirst, fever, swelling, exposure, and headache. Further pain was added through the taunting accusations of the soldiers, bystanders, religious leaders, and one thief (Matt. 27:39-44).

Despite the intense pain and unjust suffering of our Lord, He retained His spiritual integrity and expressed concern for others. The night before, when the impetuous Peter had sliced off the right ear of a temple officer, Christ had mended His enemy's wound. On the fatal cross, amid torture and animosity, Christ again displayed compassion. He prayed to the Father that His executioners might find forgiveness for their crimes; He made sure that John, the beloved disciple, and Mary, His own mother, would adopt one another as mother and son after His death; and He promised the repentant thief reunion with Him later that day in Paradise. In death, as in life, our Lord showed divine control and human sensitivity.

As that Friday lingered on, darkness eclipsed the sun (Matt. 27:45). Jesus experienced prolonged thirst and spiritual isolation from the Father. Then, with a scream, He died.

At that moment, many astonishing things happened. The temple veil was miraculously torn open; earthquakes opened old graves to reveal reviving bodies; observers at the cross confessed Christ's righteousness. But the most astounding event took place on Sunday morning, long after Jesus had been pronounced dead, wrapped, anointed, and entombed. He became alive again. As the Good Shepherd had predicted, He was able to lay down His life for the sheep and raise it up again.

What Difference Does It Make?

The death of Christ prompts us to keep our problems in perspective. However much we suffer, He has suffered more. As our High Priest who has tasted suffering and death, He understands and intercedes for us. Not only does His death pay for our sin, it gives us new life. This life begins with spiritual union with Him now and lasts into eternity. Finally, the death of Christ becomes the banner of credibility for Him to be the judge of all people. The just One will someday sit in judgment over each person in the universe (Acts 17:31). Because He has been vindicated through a righteous life, death, and resurrection, He is the One who can command repentance from all people—and enable them to find meaning even in suffering and death.

6

Why?

El Tablazo looked too close. It was approaching too fast. Exploding into the 14,000-foot peak, the DC-4 disintegrated with a metallic scream. The Avianca Airlines flight bound for Quito, Ecuador flamed crazily into the deep ravine. For one awful moment the night of a cold Columbian mountain was illuminated. Then came darkness and silence. . . .

Before leaving the airport earlier that day a young New Yorker named Glenn Chambers had scribbled a note on paper from the floor of the terminal. The scrap of paper was part of a printed advertisement which contained the single word "Why?" in the center. Chambers quickly jotted a last-minute note to his mother around that printed word, dropped it in an envelope, and into a mailbox before boarding. He assured her that there would be more to come about his lifelong dream of ministry with "Voice of the Andes" in Ecuador. . . .

But there was no more to come. Between the mailing of that final note and its delivery to Mrs. Chambers, El Tablazo had snagged his flight and life out of the night sky. The letter arrived later than the news of his death. So when the letter was opened only one question burned up at her with irony: "Why?" This is the question which comes first and lasts longest when we suffer. Why? Why me? Why now? Why this?[13]

This is perhaps the most fundamental question of life—why do suffering and trouble happen? If one's faith doesn't address the problem of human suffering, it lacks the power to interpret human experience or provide an adequate world-view.

One book of the Bible, Lamentations, deals exclusively with suffering and grief. In this small book, we find Jewish survivors of the sixth-century B.C. siege of Jerusalem asking, "Why have we suffered?" Their reflections on this subject begin our biblical response to the question of suffering.

What Did They Suffer?

In 587 B.C. Jerusalem was besieged and destroyed by the Neo-Babylonian army. Five poems describing this tragedy and the resultant grief became the Book of Lamentations. While 2 Kings 25:8-12 gives the *facts* of this national tragedy, Lamentations 1–5 provide the poetic expression and *feelings* concerning these events. As we read these poems it is obvious that the memory of fear and pain is still fresh in the survivor-writer's mind.

The grief of the poet is expressed through the Hebrew word translated as "how!" This word serves as the original title of the book as well as the opening word of three of its poems (1:1; 2:1; 4:1). It ventilates the surprise of the writer's grief and demands some reasonable explanation for his suffering. The shock of loss prompts the bereaved survivor to seek an answer to his personal tragedy; the poems seek to explain and interpret this national calamity.

The whole national community suffered greatly through its harrowing devastation. The once glorious international capital, Jerusalem, had become deserted (1:1); roads that had been filled with excited festivalgoers were now empty (1:4). Plundering enemies had become wealthy with the goods of Jerusalem (1:5), and the sacred temple had been desecrated by pagans (1:10; 2:6). In the midst of all the tragedy, there was no reliable ally to help (1:17, 4:17). In contrast, the invading soldiers seemed to get their greatest delight in observing the pain of the downtrodden survivors (1:21; 2:15). The most poignant display of national loss was seen in the corpse-littered streets of Jerusalem (2:21). A look at the faces of the dead showed that famine and war had been democratic; the dead were from all ages and both genders. In effect, the city had become a giant morgue.

In addition to community-wide suffering, there were many personal losses. People wept without anyone to console them (1:2). Children were taken as slaves (1:5). In the midst of starvation, adults traded valuable possessions for a bit of nourishment (1:11); when food could not be found, starving people began to eat the dead to survive (2:20; 4:10; Deut. 28:53). Those who did not die by famine died by the enemy's sword (1:20).

With the enemy outside the city gates, those imprisoned inside decayed physically and emotionally (3:4-9). The formerly wealthy scavenged in garbage pits for food (4:5). The once healthy and beautiful looked like walking cadavers. The most painful scenes of suffering were those between mother and child; little children begged for bread but there was none to give them (4:3-4).

Hopeless mothers caricatured themselves as being worse caregivers than the desert jackal or wilderness ostrich (4:3-4). The jackal was looked down on for barely nursing its young before thrusting them into the harsh desert, but these mothers felt they were being even more cruel to their young. Malnourished, these starving mothers couldn't even nurse their young briefly. The wilderness ostrich, on the other hand, had been stereotyped as not adequately protecting its young; it characteristically laid its eggs on the ground and left them to hatch, vulnerable to predators and travelers. The mothers of Jerusalem felt totally unable to protect their offspring from destruction. Children died in their mothers' laps (2:11-12).

Once the army was able to crash the gates and assault the city's inhabitants, new tragedies unfolded. Immediately there were rapes and hangings (5:11-12). In hours children became orphans and women became widows (5:3). People were thrown out of their homes as the occupation soldiers took over (5:2). Those who survived the takeover had to pay black market prices for drinking water and firewood (5:4). Because of the dead bodies and broken walls, packs of scavenger animals roamed city streets (5:18).

The overwhelming losses suffered by the national community and individual citizens generated intense grief. There was endless weeping (1:2, 16). It seemed that God was deaf to any prayer (3:44). It wasn't even possible to remember how it felt to be happy (3:17).

Even those who survived felt as if they were dead; they were surrounded by death and had lost all reason for living. In a cultural expression of this grief, the survivors acted out rites of mourning (2:10). They sat on the ground in silence, wore sackcloth, and threw dirt into the air and allowed it to rain down on their heads. They were, in effect, dramatically acting out their own mortality. God had said, "You are dust, and to dust you shall return" (Gen. 3:19).

Why Did They Suffer?

Anyone who has truly tasted life knows that suffering happens to all. It comes with varying degrees of intensity, frequency, and effect, but eventually comes to each of us. It was the staggering weight of the Jerusalem catastrophe that led its survivors to ask, "Why?" This age-old question reflects the instinct for self-preservation and understanding.

As one thoughtfully reads through these lament poems, it becomes apparent that *national sin* had invited suffering. Israel's unfaithfulness to God is described variously as immorality, covenant transgression, sin, and rebellion (Lam. 1:5, 8, 18, 20, 22; 4:22; 5:16). This spiritual disloyalty was considered worse than that of Sodom (4:6). It was present among all classes of people including the national leaders (4:13-16; 5:7). Even the prophets, who might have warned of the impending divine judgment for sin, had refused to expose national iniquity (2:14). Had the nation acknowledged its sin and repented, national disaster might not have occurred (2:14; 3:39-42). But instead of confessing and repenting, the nation continued in its waywardness. As a consequence, *divine anger* brought judgment in the form of an invading pagan army (1:12; 2:1-3, 6-7, 21-22; 3:1, 10; 4:11).

Judging from earlier covenant agreements (Lev. 26; Deut. 28) and from some prophetic denunciations prior to the destruction, the nation was guilty of several evils. They had left the pure worship of the Lord and had become ensnared in pagan idolatry. Besides worshiping other national deities, the

Jews had begun to depend on their own ingenuity to ensure national security; horses, kings, treaty marriages, foreign alliances, and military hardware had become the supposed guarantor of Israel's prosperity. The Lord was no longer her sole guardian and keeper, or so she thought. It was for this combination of failures that Israel was judged by the Lord through the destruction of Jerusalem.

The inspired poet of Lamentations saw God's anger and punishment as the cause of Israel's suffering. Yet he did not ignore the possibility of divine mercy within judgment. In his third lament he assures the bereaved survivors that this God who punishes for sin does not do so permanently (3:31). Rather punishment is sent to produce change in the lives of God's people. His power to cause grief matches His desire to offer compassion and loving-kindness (3:32). The Lord is described as not afflicting willingly (3:33). The sense is that the Lord's pleasure does not come from causing pain (3:33-38). If the sufferers can agree that He produces calamity, they must also acknowledge that He brings goodness, hope, and mercy (3:21-26, 38).

As a disciplining authority, the Lord is loving and consistent. Like a parent, He sets standards for His children and expects them to be obeyed. These standards are not bizarre or cruel; they are for our own good. When we break them, He inflicts consequences to reaffirm the standard and reorder our behavior.

A high school boy named Pete needed this kind of discipline. One Saturday night he talked some friends into helping steal his father's car and going for a joyride. They drove recklessly for hours. During the night Pete's father realized the car was gone and reported the theft to the police; he had no idea his son had stolen it.

Before long the police located the car on the road and arrested the thieves. When the father and the arresting officer realized at the police station what had happened, they were shocked. The officer said, "You know, if it were *my* son, I'd have to think about dropping the charges and dealing with this at home."

The father thought about it as Pete made excuses. "No, it's important that my boy face up to what he's done," the father said finally. "I wouldn't drop the charges with anybody else, and no one else would drop them if he had stolen *their* car. I love Pete, and I'll be as good to him as I can be. But he must learn from this experience so that he won't do something more foolish next time."

Pete's dad was firm, loving, and consistent. Years later Pete says, "My dad was right. I was going downhill fast. I wouldn't have learned my lesson if he had bent the rules that night. I probably would have killed myself the next time I stole a car." Pete endured some legal consequences, and the incident went on his record. But he never had a problem with the law again. Today he's a successful missionary in a large and effective ministry.

It's common to hear Pete say, "I'm glad I got caught by a father who loved me." Similarly, the people of Israel were caught in sin by the Father who loved them.

Is All Suffering Punishment for Sin?
The Book of Lamentations powerfully states that its particular national suffering was caused by divine punishment for sin. If this is sometimes the cause of human suffering, should we assume that it is *always* the cause?

Several years ago a car full of people pulled out of their church parking lot at night. Before they had arrived at the top of the first hill, a drunk driver crossed the center line and smashed into them head-on. Though there were some injuries, both drivers managed to climb out of their damaged vehicles to talk. The drunk driver, still staggering and wearing a paper party hat, managed to get out a philosophical challenge: "Tell me why this had to happen to me."

Without hesitation the sober driver responded, "I'll tell you why it happened to you. You were driving drunk on the wrong side of the road. Now you tell me: Why did it happen to *me?*"

The drunk driver had broken many laws—the law of the way his body was affected by alcohol, the laws of the highway, and the laws of the state concerning insurance and registration. His suffering which resulted from the accident might be seen as divine punishment for his wrong choices. He had reaped what he had sown (Gal. 6:7). He had broken the God-given and

57

God-supported laws that were intended to protect people. He was hurt when he defied these laws, but his suffering was the natural consequence of breaking them. In that sense his suffering was a little like that of the Jerusalem siege victims who had broken God's covenant laws.

The more delicate question is why the "innocent victims" in the church car suffered. Because there often are "innocent victims," we must enlarge on additional biblical reasons why people sometimes suffer. First, it often seems that suffering may occur to *affirm character and produce growth* (James 1:2-4; Heb. 12:1-13; 2 Cor. 12:1-10; Gen. 50:20). In this case the sufferer is not in need of correction but of development. No doubt some passengers in the second car grew in character and insight through this unwarranted and undeserved event. Similarly, many deeply mature believers have experienced suffering that gave their lives greater quality and credibility.

There are also biblical implications that suffering sometimes occurs for reasons not associated with the individual sufferer. For instance, Jesus encountered a blind man who suffered his blindness not for his own correction or development but so that God could use him *as an example to others* (John 9:1-3). Similarly, Job suffered so that God could use him as an example to instruct Satan and Job's friends (Job 1:8-12; 42:7-10). Christ did not suffer as punishment for His own sin or to teach Him new lessons; rather His suffering has its primary effect in the lives of others who take hold of His death for salvation.

A fourth possibility is that some suffering is a generic *part of life* without always having an individual purpose. When our Lord reviewed two incidents of multiple deaths, He rejected individual purposes for a generic one (Luke 13:1-5). All that could be learned from these incidents was that death occurs to all of us eventually, and we should be prepared. Though death and suffering like this may be the result of historic sin in Adam and Eve, it is not the result of personal sin in the lives of those who die. Job said, "Man is born for trouble, as sparks fly upward" (Job 5:7).

When a woman experiences the suffering associated with childbirth or a man experiences the suffering associated with manual labor (Gen. 3:16-19), no special explanation should be sought. Each is experiencing generic suffering. After my son was born and my wife had to recuperate in the hospital for nearly a week, I knew she had been through an ordeal. The ordeal had meaning and hope as all suffering does, but it was generic. I couldn't say that Nancy had experienced divine correction for her sin, that she had learned some new lesson, or that observers were moved by her heroic example. All we knew was that God's promise to uphold generic suffering in childbirth was maintained.

So what can we say about suffering?

1. It exists and touches everyone.
2. When it is severe, our instinct is to ask, "Why?"
3. Sometimes it serves to correct sin.
4. Sometimes it functions as an aid to growth.
5. Sometimes it offers an example to others.
6. Sometimes it is just a generic part of life.

Though the Bible gives sensitive and flexible alternatives for understanding suffering as a whole, it does not provide a rigid mechanism for interpreting individual cases of suffering. The sufferer should consider whether his experience can help him. It can motivate correction of his wrong behavior, affirm his positive traits, or be instrumental to others who are observing him and who are influenced by his example. It can also clarify the reality of life in a world clouded by broken ideals and laboring under the curse of sin.

Each believer who seeks to live in harmony with God's principles will have a healthy outlook—even at times of suffering and pain. The faithful believer will not allow anything to narrow his faith during suffering. He will seek to live with a clear conscience toward God and a growth pattern in his character. He will always have an interest in being a testimony to others and will be a realist about life. He may ask, "Why?" But he will also trust God even before an answer is forthcoming.

PART THREE

SUDDEN DEATH

7

Suicide

I was fueling my car at a service station near local train tracks. Suddenly I noticed several police cars pulling up without lights or sirens. The officers walked toward the tracks with whispered conversation. Then it dawned on me—another pedestrian must have been hit by a train. This was a particularly dangerous crossover; the 100-mile-per-hour train speed guaranteed accidents would be fatal.

I walked to the officers and identified myself as a minister. "Is there anything I can do?" I asked. "If there is family to be notified, I'm available to help."

An officer responded with a discouraged nod. "There is not much anybody can do right now," he said. "To the best of our knowledge a young white woman [that was all the description they had] stepped in front of that last train and committed suicide. The conductor radioed us as soon as he hit her. He was pretty shaken up because she just stepped in front of his train and stared at him. He had no chance of stopping."

There was no way to notify the family because there was no way to identify the woman. Her remains could only be found in barely recognizable fragments over several hundred yards of track. She hadn't screamed. No one had accompanied her. It was another sober, silent, lonely suicide.

Though the story of this young woman may never be fully known, it is no doubt similar to those of thirty other people who will try suicide this hour in the U.S. alone. Their stories are about feeling hopeless.

Though it can be argued that suicide is never a right choice and that felt hopelessness is never true hopelessness, despair gives some people the illusion that living is worse than dying. Suicide may seem to them to be their best option, though it is not.[14] The commonness of such feelings and actions is underscored when one considers accounts of suicide in the Bible as well as in modern society.

Suicide in the Bible

When the wicked conspirator and soldier Abimelech was seriously wounded in battle, he chose suicide to end his life (Jud. 9:50-57). A woman had thrown a large stone from atop a wall, and it had struck him in the skull and opened a tremendous wound. Rather than risking the stigma of being injured by a woman in a lost skirmish, Abimelech committed suicide on the battlefield.

When the mighty warrior-judge Samson saw his final opportunity to kill many enemy Philistines, he did so—sacrificing his own life in the process (Jud. 16:23-31). This noble act followed a life of disobedience and compromise. Just before his death, Samson had been captured by the Philistines. They blinded him, mocked him, and tied him to pillars in a public building. In a last act of desperation, Samson prayed for the strength to pull down the pillars of the festival structure. His request was granted, resulting in his death and the deaths of numerous Philistine leaders.

King Saul and his military attaché committed suicide when they were hopelessly surrounded by the pursuing Philistines (1 Sam. 31:1-6). Israel's foot soldiers had already been routed when Saul's command force was attacked; once Saul's sons lay dead around him and he had been immobilized by an enemy arrow, he feared capture and torture. He chose self-imposed death, as did his armor-bearer.

When Ahithophel's coup attempt against King David failed, he retreated to his home and hung himself (2 Sam. 17:21-23). When Zimri was hopelessly besieged by Omri's army, he burned his own house down on himself (1 Kings 16:8-20). But the best-known biblical suicide victim was Judas, Jesus' disciple. After Jesus' conviction, Judas felt guilty over his role in the arrest and trial of his former Master. The thirty pieces of silver which he had been paid for his work reminded him of his cruelty. He tried to return the money, but no one would let him reverse his bargain. Desperately alone and guilty, he hanged himself (Matt. 27:3-10; Acts 1:16-20).

Apparently with a noose around his neck, Judas jumped from a wall or tree. The initial jerk of the rope must have broken his neck. But it must also have snapped the knot, branch, or rope by which he was hanged. This is apparent since one parallel account describes his death by hanging and the other by severe internal injuries in a fall. For Judas, living with the regretful memories seemed more painful than dying at his own hands.

Evaluating the Obituaries

As one examines these seven biblical suicide incidents, some patterns emerge. First, *six of these deaths were associated with military-political incidents.* Dangerous causes often invite people who are angry or suicide-prone to "give their lives" in a blaze of glory. This pattern of last-minute military suicide among the Jews became a trademark of their pride and defiance toward the Gentiles in the Maccabean and Roman periods.

Second, *six of these people felt their deaths were imminent.* They had already suffered major injuries or feared revenge schemes would overtake them. There is no hint, however, that Judas felt his life was in danger—unless he feared Jesus' other followers or God's judgment.

Third, *suicide is never portrayed in these passages as the major issue.* The issue in each text is God's approval or disapproval of one's whole life. Each of the people in the suicide incidents had already failed morally prior to their death decisions. Previous moral faults far overshadow their suicide gestures. For instance, Saul's suicide act is far less significant in the overall narrative than are his disobedience and consultation with a medium.

Some have suggested that suicide is the "unpardonable" sin. But this notion has poor theological support.[15] The idea was proposed in the fourth century A.D. by Augustine, who reasoned that since suicide was self-murder, it was a mortal sin. Furthermore, he said, suicide did not allow time for repentance and confession of this sin after the act.

But the Bible invalidates Augustine's idea. It never discusses suicide as "unpardonable." It gives that label only to blatant blasphemy of the Holy Spirit's testimony about Jesus Christ. Furthermore, one's standing before God is determined by belief or unbelief in Jesus Christ and His saving work—not by whether one has gotten to a necessary confessional posture before death. Personal confession of sin is intended to secure a clear conscience and fellowship with God.

Fourth, *the Bible provides no actual legislation on suicide.* It does not directly address suicide either to recommend or forbid it. Should this silence be taken to mean that suicide did not exist in biblical times? This is hardly reasonable considering the foregoing examples. Does the silence imply that suicide was too taboo for public discussion? When one considers the Bible's frank discussion of incest, child sacrifice, and seances, the taboo theory seems unlikely. One could argue, however, that biblical silence implies that *suicide is never God's option.* No biblical hero of the faith ever commits suicide; no suicide act is ever condoned. When Satan dares Jesus to jump from the temple in a death-defying or death-inviting act, Jesus refuses. Instead, He predicts His death without planning or inviting it or acting out His own script.

Fifth, *suicide is a tragedy.* It ends life prematurely, unnecessarily. It disregards the worth of God's creatures who are made in His image. Since suicide, like murder, is contrary to God's support for the sanctity of life, *it should be refused at all costs.*

Sixth, *there are no clear biblical statements regarding the euthanasia or "mercy-killing" issue, which some relate to suicide.* Biblical values forbid *active* euthanasia such as poison injections, but *passive* euthanasia could be evaluated on a case-by-case basis.[16] There are times when a family has to consider withholding life support from a terminal patient who has no realistic prospect of recovery. When the patient, his family, his physician, his hospital, and local bioethical laws permit the withholding of heroic or unnecessary medical intervention, it can be considered. Medical treatments that cannot halt an illness or effectively minimize pain sometimes only prolong comatose and semi-comatose states. By most definitions this is not living.

Suicidal Feelings

Though it is essential to analyze suicide from God's perspective, it is also helpful to understand it from a human viewpoint. We must remember that people do not attempt or commit suicide for theological reasons. They do it for emotional reasons—when they feel worthless and helpless.

The problem is intensely serious. Suicide is the tenth leading cause of death in the United States and the second leading cause among U.S. college students.[17] Of the thirty attempts made this hour, three will be successful.

Depression and feelings of helplessness prompt many people to have passing thoughts about taking their own lives. This makes some of them feel more depressed and guilty because they believe strong people are not supposed to have problems, suffer defeat, or feel morbidly pessimistic. Such self-condemnation only intensifies the depression and increases the risk of suicide.

If you have ever had passing thoughts of driving into a tree or taking an overdose of tranquilizers, you are not alone. Researchers tell us that eight out of ten people report having had suicidal thoughts at some time. Severe emotional pain, unrealistic expectations, serious health problems, and major losses can lead to deep depression; if you are locked into a troubled family or enslaved by guilt, you are probably one of the 80 percent with passing fantasies of ending it all. Being very rich or very poor also makes you statistically more open to the despair which can result in suicide.

Being honest with oneself and the Lord is required in order to endure hardship and keep a spiritual and emotional balance. A person having suicidal thoughts should share them with the Lord and a mature Christian friend. When thoughts turn into an actual suicide plan, the self-destructive person needs immediately to make himself accountable to a pastor, counselor, or family member, asking directly for help and revealing the suicide plan. This disclosure is not to be made for the sake of manipulation, but only out of true need.

The depressed person who has attempted suicide in the past needs to get a handle on the factors that brought him to that point. Professional counseling will help to identify warning signals; if the victim becomes desperate, he or she should call an ambulance, hospital, or community mental health service.

The Pain of Guilt

The sad distinctive of self-destruction is that it is a uniquely human problem; animals do not commit suicide. Some aspects of God's created image in man, such as conscience and imagination, make man susceptible to paralyzing guilt or frustration when he lives outside God's will. Survival and contentment require developing a clear conscience and satisfaction with our lives before God. The truly guilty person can receive cleansing from a loving God (1 John 1:9).

One man who committed a particular sin felt so ashamed that he killed himself. When his pastor and wife read the suicide note, they were grieved to know that he did not trust their love enough to unburden himself to them. There was forgiveness available; suicide only added pain to the family and the church.

Had that man viewed his problem realistically, he would have seen that it was temporary and solvable. Most problems are, even if they don't seem so. Even his note showed his confusion—wanting to love and live, but feeling the need to die and escape. Those who struggle with guilty feelings even after confessing sin need to believe that God is greater than the human heart and knows all things (1 John 3:19-21). Self-condemnation after confession is usually caused by false guilt, Satan's attack, or the desire to do emotional penance. Time, loving relationships, and pastoral care can help turn this pattern around.

Those who have lost a loved one to suicide often live with severe pain as well. To be the bereaved survivor of a suicide victim can leave a psychological skeleton in the closet, due to guilt over not recognizing the warning signals "soon enough." Such a reaction is normal, but must be tempered by the fact that the survivor could not have *controlled* the suicide victim. All one person can do for another is to give genuine love and then trust God for the other's choices.

Relatives of suicide victims may also fear that this problem "runs in the family." But suicide is not genetic. Sometimes families or friends do develop similar escapist mentalities, however, leading to a string of suicides. Survivors of suicide victims should remember that God wants to give them strength to endure problems, not to escape from them (1 Cor. 10:13). While a loved one's taking his own life makes a survivor think about suicide more often, it does not make it right or reasonable. A domino effect need not occur. God's mercy is everlasting and extends itself to the thousandth generation; if a chain reaction is to be started, it should be one of mercy and hope.

The Power of Love
Late one night Bill came close to suicide. In tears, grasping for hope, he called a Christian friend and expressed the agony of hopelessness. In reply the friend assured him of God's love: "Bill, remember God loves you and doesn't want you to hurt yourself."

Bill pulled through that night and later became a Christian. His only regret was that he hadn't said to his friend that night: "Yes, I hear you saying that God loves me. But what I really need to hear right now is that *you* love me. Do *you* love me? Do *you* want me to live?"

Bill must have sensed the answer to those questions was yes; otherwise he wouldn't have called or rallied with hope that night. But his unasked questions remind us that we should never hesitate to affirm others personally as we assure them of God's care. God is a God of love and has called us to be a people of love—thereby helping those around us to see that there *is* a reason to live.

8

Accidents, Homicide, and the Deaths of Children

Ralph and Laurie were going out for the evening. As parents of young children they rarely had time or money to go out on a date and hire a baby-sitter, but this was a special occasion.

The baby-sitter was a responsible church friend, a high school girl who had a great way with kids. Ralph and Laurie's toddler twins were fun that night, jabbering, playing, and experimenting with their newfound skill of walking. They would crawl fast or try to trot away from the sitter, laughing. The game was "catch me if you can!"

One twin shot toward the living room while the other darted down the hall. The sitter teasingly followed the first to the living room, where she played peek-a-boo with the child for a couple of minutes. Surely the other toddler would come bouncing into the living room at any moment, the sitter thought, wanting to play peek-a-boo too. Soon the sitter swept her little playmate up, saying as she came down the hall, "Maybe your brother is hiding in the bedroom. Let's go find him."

Before they ever reached the bedroom, however, their laughter stopped. Tragedy had struck in the bathroom. The other toddler had discovered a toilet with the seat up. Reaching, splashing, leaning in, this child had slipped headfirst to a quiet death by drowning.

This death was sudden, unexpected, tragic. Could the baby-sitter have prevented this accident? Should the parents have trusted a teenager with their precious children? Would time

70

ever take away the guilt and all the "what if's" from this sudden death?

The Special Pain of Sudden Death

We grieve most at the sudden, unexpected, premature death of a loved one. When this happens through accident, criminal violence, or infant death, emotion hits us like an ocean wave. Sudden death in the immediate family always poses powerful challenges to the survivors.

Relatives and friends of a sudden-death victim often try to place the "blame" on themselves or others: "What could have been done to prevent this? What should have been done? Whose fault is it?" This reaction is illustrated in Luke 13:1-5, which mentions that a construction accident had taken the lives of eighteen men. Christ Himself argued against placing blame in this case. He insisted that the survivors get on with the more important tasks of confronting death and recovering from grief.

God is quite clear when He teaches that we all will face physical death one day (Heb. 9:27; Ecc. 3:2). But the Bible writers also capture our humanity when they describe us as wanting to live long, peaceful lives ended only by death from natural causes (Gen. 25:8). When someone dies "prematurely," we feel tense as well as sad, asking, "Why him? Why now?"

Some have died "too soon" because of their foolish choices or because of God's chastisement (1 Cor. 11:28-32; 1 John 5:16-17; 1 Sam. 2:31; Job 36:13-14; Prov. 10:21; 11:19). But any form of sudden death will stun us regardless of cause. It is extraordinary, and therefore surprising.

Our pain is especially acute when sudden death comes through violence (1 Sam. 15:32-33; 28:15-19; 1 Kings 2:28-34) or to a child (1 Kings 3:16-28; 14:17-18; 2 Kings 4:8-37). When sudden death leaves a family with no heir to carry on its heritage, there is another layer to the grief (Gen. 15:2-3; Ruth 4:10).

Unlawful Death

In the first book of the Bible a violent murder is recorded (Gen. 4). The first parents felt the shocked grief of a homicide

71

in their household. Adam and Eve had been grateful for God's gift of life when their children were born; but in one angry exchange Cain had stolen the life of his brother Abel, whose very name meant "breath."

When someone, ancient or modern, takes another's life willfully and without cause, the survivors' grief is acute and often mixed with rage. Jacqueline's mother, for example, was happily retired and living alone. From her Florida apartment she often talked on the phone with her children and grandchildren. One Sunday she called her daughter in Maryland, not knowing it would be her last such conversation.

One hour later there was a knock at her door. She opened it, a gunshot rang out, and a bullet passed through the storm door and into her heart. Apparently the attacker turned and fled. Jacqueline's mother, mortally wounded, staggered back a few steps into her living room and fell in a kneeling position beside the sofa, where she died.

The family of Jacqueline's mother was angry and confused over the cruelty and vague motive of the unknown killer. Would this confusion and anger become destructive and habitual? Would family and friends be able to believe that the murderer was not lurking behind every corner, stalking them? Would they be able to go on living as their mother would have wanted without becoming absorbed in the police manhunt?

To date investigators have not found the murderer or learned of a motive for the crime. But Jacqueline and her family have learned some lessons. They have learned from the Apostle John that this murderer, like all others, had Cain as a model and was characterized by evil deeds (1 John 3:11-15). But rather than imitating the killer's evil and becoming addicted to destructive anger, the Christians in this family have learned to love more deeply. Their genuine love for God and man has become the proof of their faith.

The Deaths of Children

One of the most difficult tragedies to accept is the death of a child. Even mature, well-balanced adults have become bitterly disillusioned over such seemingly ill-timed deaths. This was the case with a former coworker of mine, who had spent the first three years of our working relationship making critical and emotional condemnations about religion. It was only after a long, personal discussion that he told me why. He had turned from religion after a young neighbor girl had succumbed to leukemia. It seemed to him that if God existed at all, He was either too weak or too cruel to stop such tragedies; it wasn't worth believing in a God like that, he said.

Carl Jung said that the death of a child is like a period before the end of a sentence—sometimes when the sentence has barely begun. As we recall the biblical metaphor of life as a blossoming flower, it almost seems when a child dies that God has plucked the flower bud before it has had the chance to bloom. It is this kind of painful loss which King David underwent.

David, the Grieving Parent

David, king in Jerusalem, had committed sexual sin with Bathsheba. Her pregnancy set off a string of cover-ups, beginning with multiple lies about the extramarital affair—and ending in the murder of Uriah, her husband, under the guise of battle. David felt he had hidden his sin effectively, but the Lord sent Nathan the prophet to confront the King about his actions (2 Sam. 12:1-25). The message of prophetic judgment declared that the child of this illegimate affair would die. Though the child was in no way cited as a guilty party in the parents' sin, a prediction about his early illness and death was offered before his birth as a sign to David. The sign showed God's awareness of David's sins and served as their painful consequence.

Immediately after the birth, David learned of his child's acute illness. Perhaps David had thought the birth could be kept quiet for several months, but the infant's sickness and death would bring the news of illegitimacy to the royal subjects. Then, informed of his son's terminal condition, David began to grieve (2 Sam. 12:16-18). For a week, while his child hung between life and death, David wept, prayed, and denied himself life's necessities. He didn't eat or sleep as he begged God's mercy for him and his family. All the normal parental instincts to nurture and protect one's offspring were exercised, but David was helpless to intervene.

David's grief was so intense that week that his attendants feared news of the child's death might move David to commit suicide (2 Sam. 12:18). But the opposite was true. When the child died, David began to reinvest in life. He bathed, dressed, ate, and began comforting Bathsheba. Death had come to David's home, but he was beginning the slow road back to normalcy.

A Slow Road Indeed

We should not conclude that David's experience mandates a one-week grieving period for parents who lose children. Because the death of a child continues to represent different losses during all the stages of life, the potential for prolonged grief and depression is great. When a father has lost his baby son, for example, he is likely to relive the grief years later when he drives past a Little League game and has no boy to root for. The same father might also relive his grief on what would have been his son's sixteenth birthday, picturing the two of them buying and rebuilding an old car. Even when that father retires and wants to leave his company in good hands or needs a strong man to help maintain his house, the grief can be resurrected.

Attachment to children can have so many layers of meaning that one's grief can become overwhelming as well as prolonged. Obsession with the deceased child can result; so can clinical, chronic depression. Because of these special challenges, joining an organized support group like Compassionate Friends can be a good idea for many bereaved parents.

"Are We Responsible?"

Since the Bible specifically states that David's son died because of David's sin, we face an additional consideration. Are parents responsible for their children's deaths? Do parents' sins cause children to die?

I am convinced that most parents are not morally responsible for their children's deaths. There is no connection in most cases between a parent's behavior and a child's death, though in other cases parents do abort their children before birth, or cause death through abuse after birth. God can forgive even these sins, however, as Christ forgave the Roman soldiers who crucified Him. God can forgive parents who sin against their children.

Yet most parents feel psychologically responsible for their children's deaths, even when they are not morally responsible. Because they possess the God-given instinct to nurture and protect, most parents feel responsible for everything that happens to their children. They feel responsible for the bullies at the playground who beat up their sons and daughters. They feel responsible for the hit-and-run drivers who run over their children. They feel responsible for the wars that take the lives of their sons.

As a result most bereaved parents experience a penitential quality to their grief before they heal. Thus bereaved parents must be helped to cope so that their grief does not turn into a distorted, guilt-induced depression.

Infections in the Grief Wound

The initial challenge of acute grief is to survive the first months. The bereaved parent may feel as if he or she has been sliced open with a sharp knife and is bleeding profusely. There are no quick-fix tourniquets, however; the parent needs to look squarely at the wound and start washing it by being honest with himself about what has happened.

Next the parent needs support from others, to express grief and let others express theirs. Soon, as if using a sore arm, the bereaved person must start caring for himself and reaching out to others, even though it will hurt and feel awkward.

After the acute phase of grief is over, a parent may be pulling together outwardly while some "germs" are creeping into the old wound. The three main infecting agents are guilt, anger, and depression. A guilty parent can make himself the scapegoat in a child's death, sometimes resulting in divorce, suicide, alcoholism, or other forms of self-destruction.

Prolonged anger can lead to a fierce assault on a "culprit"— God, a doctor, a baby-sitter, or a drunk driver. If such action can protect other innocent people, it may be worthwhile. But the angry parent will never get his child back. The bereaved parent needs to heal, not to become obsessed with lawsuits and punitive social activism.

Prolonged depression can paralyze a parent and keep him from functioning. Consequently he may lose his job, his health, or important relationships. All of these are needed for the healing task.

Hope for Parents

After his son died, King David displayed more than family grief. He displayed family hope as well (2 Sam. 12:20-25). He said, "I shall go to him, but he will not return to me" (2 Sam. 12:23). David accepted the reality of physical separation in death, but I believe he expected to be reunited with his son in the afterlife.

David's hope of reunion was not based on infant baptism, occult communication, reincarnation, or purgatory. Instead, I believe he expected to one day be present with the personal, departed spirits of all children and righteous adults. This reunion included being with his own son.

When our Lord taught about children (Matt. 18:1-14; 19:13-15), I believe there were literal children with Him as object lessons. He taught with a child on His lap and said that the kingdom was made up of people like these children. He taught that, like children, we must have simple faith. Furthermore, we should humbly value spiritual and physical children; He taught that spiritual greatness is not based on who notices us but on whom we notice, such as inconspicuous children.

As seen in Matthew 18:10, Jesus taught that the spirits of children are in the presence of God. It seems that the Greek word *angelos* ("angel" or "spirit") in this verse does not refer to the guardian angel of a living child. Rather it refers to the departed spirit of a deceased child. *Angelos* was used frequently to refer to departed spirits in Jewish writings such as Matthew's Gospel. The same word is used this way in Acts 12:15, when a girl thought she had seen Peter's "ghost" (*angelos*), signifying to her that he had died. Instead it was Peter alive in bodily form. In the Acts passage, *angelos* carries the idea of departed spirit and not guardian angel. Thus the teaching in Matthew seems to be that since God welcomes little children in death, we ought to welcome and value them in life.

Biblically we know that Christ paid for all of human sin (John 1:29; 1 John 2:1-2). Though a child technically shares in Adam's sin and may suffer physical death, a newborn such as David's could not sin by personal choice. Furthermore, a young child can die before choosing to believe or disbelieve in Christ. In such a case, it is only God's grace through Christ which protects this child. When David's one-week-old baby died, genuine personal faith by that child was impossible; but because of Christ's death and God's foreknowledge, David's child exited this life into the presence of the Lord.

The bereaved king of Israel lived toward reunion with this child. We, like David, can anticipate a future eternal day when death will no longer abbreviate the lives of children or plague the human race through accidents, homicides, or other means (Isa. 65:17-25).

PART FOUR

OLD AGE

9

The Silver Cord

Recently I visited a patient in a nursing home. While I was there, the man's 90-year-old roommate frequently asked for assistance. He needed to be lifted out of bed and into bed, to be covered with blankets or uncovered, to be provided the basic necessities of life. Old age and physical degeneration had left him highly dependent, frustrated, and weary of life. Just hours after we cared for this elderly man, he died in his sleep.

Solomon described this life-weary stage in Ecclesiastes 12:1. This key verse challenges us to invest ourselves in knowing God the Creator throughout life, "Before the evil days come and the years draw near when you will say 'I have no delight in them.' " Certainly Solomon was not saying acute old age and physical deterioration are evil in a moral sense; rather they can be troubled and difficult. Old age can be a time of frustration and lack of pleasure. For some people who have to live at this threshold of eternity, the world can become a bothersome place.

Why Not Wait?

Why does Solomon advocate knowing God from youth on, especially in light of old age? Is he naive enough to think that faith keeps us from getting old and dying? Certainly not. Does he propose that a spiritual foundation in life will keep the elderly person from feeling time-weary and physically shack-

81

led? Perhaps even this is unreasonable. Possibly Solomon is saying that old age is often a time of remembering and regretting; one of the ways to minimize the painful regret of old age is to live by an eternal value system throughout life.

Another possible reason for Solomon's advice is that people can become more inflexible in later life. He sees the older person who has always denied God becoming more resistant to Him during the final years. Thus it is best to plant the seeds of spiritual life in childhood and early adulthood, so that they can grow into strong oaks. It is usually more difficult to plant seeds in hardened soil.

In the Book of Ecclesiastes Solomon traces his own pilgrimage. He had pursued both wisdom and folly (1:17), tasting every philosophy of life. This earlier hybrid approach is detailed in Ecclesiastes 1–11, resulting in both melancholy satire and sober wisdom about aging and death. It is in Ecclesiastes 12 that he reaffirms his life-tested perspective on wisdom.

What It's Like to Get Older

In Ecclesiastes 12 Solomon insightfully describes old age and death through metaphors.[18] The following table lists these metaphors and their apparent meanings:

Solomon's Description	Analogy to Old Age and Death
v. 1 Evil days	Life seems more troublesome and obstructed than before
Delightless years	Life seems to provide fewer celebrations and reasons for living
v. 2 Sun, light, moon, stars darkened	Clear weather is passing, signaling the autumn of life
Storm clouds come	The onset of winter signals the tapering off of life

v. 3 Watchmen of the house tremble — The hands shake with weakness

Mighty men stoop over — The posture is hunched

Grinders at the mill quit because there are so few of them — Chewing is diminished since many teeth have fallen out

Those who gaze through windows grow dim — Eyesight deteriorates

v. 4 Doors that used to open onto the street are shut; there is little activity inside — The mouth is usually shut; not much is said or eaten

Someone sleeping wakes up at the sound of a bird singing — Sleep is easily interrupted

The daughters of song sing more softly than they used to — Hearing deteriorates

v. 5 Men are afraid of high places — Balancing on a ladder or chair seems more dangerous

Men are afraid of terrors on the road — The dangers of travel are more terrifying

The almond tree blossoms — The hair turns gray or white

The grasshopper drags himself along — Movement is more labored and slow

The caperberry is ineffective — Sexual response is less potent

Man goes to his eternal home	The person dies and goes to his eternal destiny
Mourners go about in the streets	The body is carried through the streets among mourners
v. 6 The silver cord is broken	The hanging braid of an oriental lamp is cut; the light goes out; life ends
The golden bowl is crushed	The pottery lamp itself is broken; the light goes out; life ends
The pitcher by the well is shattered	The water jug is broken; water is cut off; life ends
The wheel at the cistern is crushed	The pulley for the well is destroyed; water is cut off, life ends
v. 7 The dust returns to the earth	The body decomposes
The spirit returns to God who gave it	The immaterial person meets God

Solomon's metaphors are picturesque and specific. They leave us with a composite image of the "aging trajectory." But it is important to realize that not every person will experience every one of these traits, nor will all experience them to the extreme. Many people will not even reach this stage in life. Even those whose systems wear down gradually may not suffer the total deterioration Solomon described. It is essential to be sensitive to *individual* adults; when we stereotype all "old people," we display a class prejudice called "ageism."

This kind of prejudice was shown in a recent survey.[19] Most of the respondents made the following generalizations about the elderly: that they cannot learn; that they have no sexual interest or activity; that they do not want to work; and that they like to be helpless. It would do those survey respondents, as well as the rest of us, some good to remember a few feats people have accomplished late in their lives:[20]

- George Bernard Shaw wrote his first play at age 48.
- Sophocles wrote *Oedipus Rex* at age 75.
- Freud wrote his last book at age 83.
- Pope John XXIII was elected at age 77.
- Benjamin Franklin invented the bifocal lens at age 78.
- Coco Chanel reentered the world of fashion at age 72.
- Bertrand Russell formed the Committee of 100, an organization devoted to nuclear disarmament, at age 88.
- John Wayne won an Oscar at age 62.
- Michelangelo created St. Peter's and frescoed the Pauline Chapel between ages 71 and 89.
- Mahatma Gandhi launched the Quit India movement, leading to India's independence, at age 72.
- Frank Lloyd Wright completed the Guggenheim Museum at age 91.
- George Burns launched a new movie career, winning an Oscar at age 80.
- Cecil B. DeMille produced *The Ten Commandments* at age 75.
- Claude Monet began his Water Lily series at age 73.
- Charles de Gaulle returned to power in France at age 68.

Compassion for the Elderly

We shouldn't overuse Solomon's metaphors of old age, but we shouldn't ignore them either. In these figures of speech Solomon has laid out an agenda for compassionate ministry to the aged. How sensitive are you to the losses and potential depression of an older person? (v. 1) Are you able to affirm an old man even though he no longer has the strength and posture which once made him proud? (v. 3) What about the foods you serve the elderly, the literature you give them, the little jobs you could do for them? (vv. 3, 5) Would you consider helping someone get reading glasses, a large-print book, a hearing aid, or wheelchair access to your church or home? (vv. 3-5) If you are a younger person, how are your senses and body functions? Do you take them for granted? Do you jeopardize them by "living dangerously"? In other words, do you have a wise perspective on the divinely created body and its built-in aging process?

God would have us age well and care well for the elderly among us. He would also have us hear Solomon's critique of lifestyles which take life, health, or youthful energy for granted. Rather than abusing or jeopardizing these God-given privileges, we should begin living with time-tested eternal values today.

Keeping Old Age Positive

The older person can do several things to heed Solomon's advice and keep his outlook positive and lively. First, he or she can become involved with a "senior-sensitive" church—one which sponsors gatherings just for senior adults as well as for all ages. Leaders of this church will look to the older adult for help in ministry, including short-term missions. This church will also seek to help needy seniors with meals, visits, transportation, and companionship.

The older adult can also cultivate his physical and emotional health. Proper hygiene and nutrition enhance well-being at any age. Many older adults are tempted to retreat in these areas once they lose their key companions or family involvement, but keeping clean, dressing up, and eating well are as important as they ever were. To further protect health, the older person should exercise regularly; many men and women have enjoyed regular walking, cycling, or group exercise classes. Sometimes recreation also provides the companionship of others who are participating.

Older men and women can also make this phase more positive by remaining as active as possible. Many senior adults find part-time or volunteer work, traveling, or exploring the resources of libraries and craft shops to be highly satisfying. Those who live alone should learn to use the radio, TV, and telephone as barriers against depressive isolation, and learn to use public or senior-centered transportation to avoid being locked into their houses.

Solomon's Symbols of Death

Before leaving Solomon's list of metaphors, we should examine two well-known but incorrect understandings of Ecclesiastes 12:6. The "silver cord" has been interpreted as the *spinal cord* by people trying to find a corresponding body part. This seems odd since few spinal cords break in old age or death. Furthermore, it seems unnecessary since the metaphors of Ecclesiastes 12:1-7 do not always refer to a specific body part; witness the clouds returning after the rain in 12:2, for example. All the context requires is that the metaphor refer to some aspect of the aging or dying person.

A second, more disturbing interpretation has been that the "silver cord" is a *light-rope of energy* connecting the physical head to a disembodied spiritual head. This view has been proposed by psychics and those who practice astral projection—the art of leaving the body at will in trancelike spiritual journeys.[21] Though it is not our purpose here to evaluate and refute such occult ideas, we can affirm that true absence from the body is to be in the postmortem presence of the Lord (2 Cor. 5:8). Furthermore, the reference to the "silver cord" in Ecclesiastes 12:6 is nestled between obvious descriptions of physical death in 12:5 and 12:7. Simply following the train of thought would suggest a reference to normal physical death, not an alleged psychic event which could happen at an earlier age.

Some historical information can also be helpful in deciphering this metaphor. Many homes in Solomon's day and region were lit by pottery lamps, each of which was suspended by a macrame-like cord. When these lamps were lit, the household was full of life and activity. When they were extinguished or destroyed, the home fell into darkness and inactivity. This darkness figuratively describes physical death.

Anyone who objects to drawing "silver cord" and "golden bowl" into one metaphor of the oriental lamp should observe 12:6. Here two parallel terms, "pitcher by the well" and "wheel at the cistern," are drawn together into one metaphor of the water source. When the *light* of life or the *water* of life is cut off, physical death is pictured.[22]

For Us Today

Solomon's teaching on old age and death challenges us to face death, not deny it. We should live, not with a morbid preoccupation about death, but with a healthy consciousness that we are finite creatures. Only the Creator can give us this proper perspective on life now and life to come. Among those who work closely with dying patients, it has been noted that those patients who develop strong religious beliefs before the crises of old age, physical deterioration, and death are the ones who make superior adjustments to the crises when they come.[23]

It is little wonder that we are urged to redeem the time (Eph. 5:16) in light of physical death. In the words of the wise and aged King Solomon, "Remember also your Creator. . . . Fear God and keep His commandments, because this applies to every person. Because God will bring every act to judgment, everything which is hidden, whether it is good or evil" (Ecc. 12:1, 13-14).

10

The Example of Joseph

I admire the person who is successful—who lives life skillfully. When someone can combine the best of human integrity and creativity with an intense consciousness of God, I offer him the title "great." The Hebrew patriarch Joseph was just such a person. He is one of the few people in Scripture to whom much narrative is devoted—but about whom nothing negative is ever said.

Joseph's View of Life
I believe Joseph was great for two reasons: He had a godly view of life and a godly view of death. We see the former in his ability to cope with injustice; sold as a slave by his brothers, accused of rape by Potiphar's wife, and forgotten in prison by the official cupbearer, Joseph did not become bitter and vengeful (Gen. 37–50). In fact, quite the opposite happened. When he rose to prominence he had the authority to execute any form of revenge he wished. Instead he chose to see God's hand even in his troubles. He said to his brothers, "As for you, you meant evil against me, but God meant it for good" (Gen. 50:20).

Even in Joseph's most desperate circumstances he could still believe God would bring about something good through his suffering. Isn't this what we see so often in the Bible and in life? Was the tragedy of Jesus' death without any lasting benefit? (1 Cor. 1:18; 2:8) If Stephen hadn't been murdered, would the early church have been scattered as missionaries to the whole known world? (Acts 7:54–8:4) If Wycliffe missionary Chet Bitterman hadn't been martyred in Colombia, would there have been a subsequent Colombian revival?

As you look back over your life with the perspective of Joseph, what good can you see coming from your own suffering? Are you willing to see even the intentional harm done against you as producing something good? Is your God larger than fate and wiser than chance? As a believer you can be confident that God is on your side to develop your Christian character (Phil. 1:6; Rom. 8:23–31). He wants you to succeed as Joseph did by having a godly view of life.

Joseph's View of Old Age and Death

Joseph also exhibited unusual wisdom concerning old age and death. This quality can be seen in ten of his traits:

1. *Joseph loved and honored his elderly father Jacob.* Unlike many in our youth-oriented society, Joseph could see the value of an elderly person. He showed his affection for his father publicly by embracing him (Gen. 46:29). Joseph was not embarrassed to introduce his father to important people like the Pharaoh (Gen. 46:31). Even when the elderly Jacob expressed negative attitudes, Joseph still loved and honored him (Gen. 47:9).

This was the challenge faced by a man we'll call Alan. His father had been in a veterans' hospital for years, having suffered a major head trauma in Italy during World War II and developed a neurological disorder. The elderly father's illness was chronic and his behavior could border on the bizarre. Whether his medications helped him was never quite clear, but they did seem to leave him depressed.

Alan sometimes wondered if it was worth it to make the long visits to see his dad. There were times when his father didn't respond to him, welcome him, or even recognize him. But he and other family members continued to visit, call, and write.

One afternoon after Alan and his father had gone off the hospital grounds for lunch, they walked back into the ward in a positive mood. It was time for Alan to leave. With a nurse standing nearby, Alan turned to his father to say good-bye. The elderly man offered a handshake, but Alan turned it into a quick hug, saying, "I love you, Dad."

His father, not comfortable with affection, stuttered, "I . . . I . . . uh." The nurse prompted him, "Come on, Mr. Washington. Tell your son you love him. You've had a good visit today." This time the elderly man said weakly, "I . . . I . . . me too! Thanks." And then he was off to his dayroom.

It was important for Alan to give his elderly father unconditional love and respect. Alan could not base his relationship to his father on his father's responses; those were too erratic. Alan could not say, "If you meet my needs, I'll meet some of yours." After all, when Alan was a child his father had sought to meet Alan's needs without demanding perfect and rewarding responses. It made sense now for Alan to show love and respect to his elderly father, even if the rewards were unpredictable.

Our attitudes about death usually surface around those who are severely ill or aged. They remind us of our own mortality. We should therefore examine our behavior and feelings around sick, aged, or dying relatives; our reactions may serve as barometers for our attitudes toward our own aging and deaths.

2. *Joseph provided for his father's physical needs in old age.* Joseph delighted in being able to share his possessions with his reunited family (Gen. 47:12). He no doubt felt a little odd, as we do when we see our parents become dependent on us after they have been the providers for years. But Joseph could make the adjustment because he was generous to others, grateful for what he had, and tolerant of the aging and dying process which is in all of us—even in our once-strong parents.

While this principle does not require all elderly parents to have identical care, it does suggest that when possible they should have the same quality of care that Joseph gave. This includes meeting physical needs, speaking freely with each other, and being supportive as a family.

Tragically, few modern American families take pride in meeting the needs of older family members. It is common today to hear even of elder abuse; older people are often defrauded financially, harassed verbally, and frightened into social isolation.

Not long ago a young man was executed for a horrible crime against an elderly relative, a widow who lived alone. This man had broken into the woman's home and raped her. Then after beating her savagely, he tied and nailed her to a wooden chair. Finally he mocked her, shot her, and set her on fire. Later he confessed to this unimaginably cruel elder abuse. His crime is most clearly rebuked by the godly and wholesome example of Joseph.

3. *Joseph conversed openly with his father about death and disposition.* It must have been hard for Joseph to accept losing his father in death. He had already lost his mother years before as a boy, and had been separated from his father for most of his adult life. But when it seemed death was coming and Jacob wanted to discuss burial arrangements, Joseph was involved and supportive (Gen. 47:29-31). Jacob wanted to be buried in the Cave of Machpelah where his wife Leah, his parents Isaac and Rebekah, and grandparents Abraham and Sarah were already buried. Joseph honored Jacob's desire to discuss this difficult subject.

Often adult children must let the aged or dying parent dictate the level at which death and disposition will be discussed. In some families such a conversation will be continued for several months; in others it will be discussed clearly and then laid aside for more important matters of saying good-bye. In no case should adult sons or daughters force a conspiracy of silence because they think they are protecting the family. They are probably protecting themselves from the pain of adjustment and preparatory grief.

It is special that Jacob described his own death as "when I lie down with my fathers" (47:30) and being "gathered to my people" (49:29). Though the concept of life after death is expressed very faintly at this point, there seems to be tender anticipation of reunion with deceased kin. It is implied that Jacob will do more than live on in the memory of those who knew him, or in his physical offspring. The phrases hint at some personal existence and conscious identity with a larger clan or family. Many members of this larger clan were already deceased.

4. *Joseph valued the role of grandparents.* Joseph sought Jacob to elicit his blessing on grandsons Ephraim and Manasseh (Gen. 48:1). According to this custom, the oldest male in the clan would speak for the whole family and for the Lord in

characterizing the child and his destiny. It was during this grandfatherly pronouncement that Jacob said his grandsons were like sons to him (48:5). Yet there were not just the normal congratulations. Instead Jacob spoke prophetically by reversing the grandsons' order for blessings (Gen. 48:8-20),

Though our customs may not match those of Joseph's day, this experience can encourage us to responsibly involve grandparents in the raising of children. Grandparents are not to be seen as mere ornaments of tradition or relics of the past, but rather as contributing members to the identity and health of the family.

5. *Joseph participated in the making and use of a will.* From his deathbed, Jacob distributed his authority and possessions among his inheritors (Gen. 48:21-22; 49:1-33). In essence, he was giving his last will and testament to his family.[24]

The example of Jacob and Joseph encourages us to be good stewards of our possessions and influence, giving some precedent for the use of wills and perhaps of life insurance. Their example certainly advocates clear communication at this time of family transition.

6. *Joseph looked toward the future with hope.* In the accounts of Jacob's and Joseph's deaths, there is a forward look. The two men focused not merely on past losses but also on future prospects. This is illustrated by the hope of reunion with kin and the desire to be reassociated with the Promised Land (Gen. 48:21; 49:29-30). Joseph's explicit instructions about the disposition of his remains included an anticipation of the national exodus from Egypt (Gen. 50:24-25).

Though Joseph's example teaches us about the pain of loss, it balances the loss with optimism about what is to come. As a Greek philosopher once said, "As the physical eyesight declines, the spiritual eyesight improves." This positive spiritual vision was characteristic of Joseph. Like him, we are to be a people who grieve—but with hope (1 Thes. 4:13).

7. *Joseph grieved candidly.* At the time of Jacob's death, Joseph expressed his grief openly and honestly. He embraced his father, kissed him, wept over him, and gave him a royal funeral and cortege. In fact, the special treatment of forty days for embalming and seventy days for national sorrow accorded Jacob was reserved only for heads of state and other dignitaries.

In these gestures of sorrow, Joseph communicated the whole-someness and normalcy of candid grief. The social taboo so prevalent in our day that strong people do not visibly grieve is contradicted by Joseph's behavior.

8. *Joseph rejected pagan funeral practices.* When Joseph turned to the mortuary professionals of Egypt, known as the magicians or embalmers, he saw the rampant paganism associated with their trade. He knew about the Egyptian myths of Osiris, Isis, and Set and the superstitous fears and practices contained in *The Egyptian Book of the Dead.* When Joseph considered the drastic differences between his family's faith and the beliefs of the sorcerer priests, he chose the "physicians" to do the embalming (Gen. 50:2). These professionals were skilled in medicine. Thus Joseph avoided pagan superstition and craft.[25]

Joseph did accept some wholesome cultural patterns that were common to Egypt, however. He made use of mummification, closing the deceased's eyes, a large procession, a coffin, and the practice of not coming into the direct presence of Pharaoh (Gen. 46:4; 50:1-4, 9, 26). Joseph's choices demonstrate that it is a matter of preference as to how one handles the funeral of a loved one. We are only encouraged to avoid direct associations with a pagan view of death.

9. *Joseph honored his father's last request.* Joseph not only conversed with his father at the end of Jacob's life (Gen. 49:29-33), but he also remembered his promises and followed through on them (Gen. 50:4-14). Joseph was not a son who did only what was convenient for his aged and dying father. Rather he listened well and kept commitments he had made. He is an encouragement to us to be responsible, consistent companions to our dying relatives, not just passive spectators.

10. *Joseph imitated his father's character qualities.* When Jacob died, Joseph had the perfect opportunity to seek revenge against his brothers without upsetting his father (Gen. 50:15-21). The brothers had truly wronged Joseph by threatening his life and selling him as a slave. Furthermore, God had affirmed Joseph's supremacy through the vision of stars and sheaves (Gen. 37:5-11). Had Joseph been looking for grounds for revenge, he could have found it. Instead he tenderly forgave his brothers.

Joseph did not just pretend to care for his brothers while Jacob was alive, thinking this would impress Jacob and ensure his favoritism. Instead, the loyalty, love, and forgiveness that characterized Jacob's final years were only expanded on by Joseph. Clearly Joseph's bond with his father extended beyond mere blood or inheritance ties; he truly mirrored the character qualities which would please his father.

The Book of Genesis is a book of contrasts, opening with Creation in a beautiful garden and ending with the bones of Joseph in a coffin in Egypt. The book shows how aging and death entered the human drama. But in one of its main characters, Joseph, we have a model for wholesome relationships and future hopes.

PART FIVE

LOOKING TO THE FUTURE

11

Helping Children Understand Death

David, a third-grader, had tears in his eyes as he stood at the casket of his grandfather, who had died earlier that week. All the adults around him were talking quietly; some wiped their eyes with handkerchiefs. The constant organ music and profusion of flowers seemed strange to him. He had never been at a viewing before nor seen a dead person.

David felt mostly sad, because his mother was crying. He had so many questions to ask, but his father had warned him how to behave at the funeral home: "Now, David, you need to be strong tonight. Your mother doesn't need to see you bawling. It's hard enough for her, as it is for Grandma. The men have to be strong. And make sure you don't get noisy there tonight; it is a very serious time. And when you get home, don't go crying to your room. Your little brother and sister need you to be an example to them." So there David stood like a little soldier, his mind racing with questions.

Soon David saw his mother sit on a folding chair, so he went to join her. "Mom, don't be so sad," he said. "Oh, I'm not sad, David," she replied. "Sometimes people cry when they are happy. You know, the Bible says Grandpa is in heaven now and we're happy for him."

"But why did he go to heaven, Mom?" David shot back.

"Because God loved him and took him to heaven, that's why. When God loves you and you love Him, He takes you to heaven when you die." At that David's mother rose to her feet to greet another guest. David sat alone, repeating to himself the words of his mother, trying to understand. He felt a little hungry and was getting tired of that room. Finally, after three hours, David and his family went home.

They ate a late supper when they got there, and the children headed to bed. David's father suggested the children sing a Sunday School song, and then he would pray before they went to sleep. The littlest one started singing, "Jesus loves me this I know. . . ." Everyone sang the song but David, whose face was sober. Then he blurted, "I don't want God to love me. I don't want to go to heaven. I don't want to die!"

David began to cry loudly. It took his father a while to calm him down and explain that Grandpa had died because he was very old and had cancer. "Grandpa didn't die just because God loved him," David's father said. "God loves us all. You don't have to worry about dying. You have a healthy body." It took a while to talk out David's misunderstanding. Though the episode was traumatic, talking helped all of them—even Dad. They exchanged hugs, prayed, and went to sleep.

Through a Child's Eyes

David's parents could be commended for some of their efforts to help him understand death. But they also could have greatly improved their tries at death education.

It was good for his parents to allow David to participate in the viewing, since he wanted that. It was good to talk with him at various points during the day, eventually allowing him to reveal his confusion over why his grandfather died. But his parents should have explained to David in detail what he would see and how people would behave at the funeral home. An adult should have stayed with him at all times, allowing him to ask questions as he had them.

The parents also should have told the children the truth during previous months concerning the grandfather having cancer. He had been in and out of the hospital and was clearly dying. But the children had been told, "Grandpa is on vacation." They had never gotten to say good-bye to him or to hear why he had died. In addition, David's father should never have burdened the boy with the idea of being unemotional and with the unrealistic task of protecting his mother and siblings from grief. Grief needs to be expressed and shared among the survivors for proper healing.

Perhaps the most problematic exchange came when David sat with his mother. He was trying to keep her from being sad, an unrealistic and unhealthy goal for a child. When David tried to find out why his grandfather had died, his mother avoided the question. She preferred to deny her grief and act as though she was crying out of happiness over her father's heavenly home.

David had asked why his grandfather had died. In other words, why had he died and not stayed alive? Why is it that people die? Why might we die? But his mother wasn't really listening; she felt the need to use religious clichés. She should have said something like, "David, Grandpa died because he was very old and had a disease called cancer. None of the rest of us has cancer. We will probably never get it—or if we do, it will probably be when we are very, very old. A lot of times the doctors can cure cancer, but they couldn't with Grandpa."

Instead of answering him factually, however, David's mother used abstractions. She acted as though David had asked, "Does God love Grandpa or not? Did Grandpa go to heaven or not?" While these questions may have been very important to David, he wanted to know why Grandpa had died, why other family members might die, why *he* might die. When the answer came, "Because God loved him," David's fear started. If Grandpa had died only because God loved him, then David was afraid of God's love.

As David's family discovered, good death education is needed to prevent the confusion and panic many people experience when death touches a loved one. In fact, mortality is like sexuality, in that it touches virtually every phase of our lives, and demands preparation for the transitions it brings. Imagine the fears and misconceptions a child will have at the onset of puberty if he or she has heard little or nothing about sex. Worse yet, consider a bride or groom who approaches the wedding night with only a child's knowledge of sexuality. Similarly, young David had to endure the death of his grandfather without sound preparation.

101

Guidelines for Death Education with Children

Here are some simple guidelines parents can use to teach children about death:

First, *use available object lessons*. Often an alert parent can introduce basic concepts of aging, loss, and grief to his child by referring to the death of a pet, a TV actor, or a public figure. This preparation helps the child face the loss of a friend, sibling, grandparent, or parent.

Object lessons are abundant in every yard or park. In our yard, for example, I chopped down several trees which had died of old age. This gave me the opportunity to talk to my son Ryan about trees that are alive and trees that are dead. I helped him learn how to distinguish between the two. We also became comfortable using the word "dead" because we weren't very attached to those trees. Over a period of days while we worked, we talked through the life cycle of a tree and compared it with a human life.

Any adult could do this, telling the story of a tree to a child and using it as an object lesson. The story might go like this: "Do you have a favorite tree in your yard or in your neighborhood? If you do, you know it is alive and growing. Do you know the story of the tree? Well, the story goes like this. A long time ago somebody put a seed in the ground. The seed grew and became a little tree. Later the tree grew bright green leaves during the spring and summer. In the fall its leaves turned yellow, red, orange, and purple. It was a beautiful tree. But then the leaves began to fall off in the windy days before winter. By Thanksgiving the branches were all empty. By Christmas the tree was chilly and covered with snow. The leaves died. They stopped living and growing. They became a part of the dirt on the ground. We say good-bye to the leaves. Many years from now the tree will also die. It will stop growing and fall down on the ground. It will become a part of the dirt on the ground. We will say good-bye to the tree."

Second, *accept individual differences among children as to how much they can and want to understand*.[26] In general, children who are three years old or younger have no concept of death other than absence. To them the dead person is gone as a father might be gone when he is at work. Between ages three and five, most children can see death as something that happens—but without pattern or finality. As far as they are concerned, death happens to some people at some times but isn't permanent; the dead person can stop being dead just as people can awake from sleep or return from a trip. An example of this took place after President John F. Kennedy's funeral. After young John-John Kennedy had spent the whole day in public mourning for his father, he asked, "When is Daddy coming home?" He thought physical death was temporary.

A child between the ages of five and nine can usually understand that death happens to some people and is final. But he does not necessarily recognize that death eventually happens to all people, including himself. Generally a child who is nine years old or more can grasp the concept that death is final, inevitable, universal, and personal.

Third, *look for a variety of emotional responses to bereavement*. We should help children express their grief, but not assume that all bereaved children will demonstrate their grief in the same ways. A parent should be alert for many different reactions including denial, physical distress, hostility, guilt, replacement, identification, and idealization.

Tracy's father had died. The funeral had been held earlier in the day, and now friends were at the bereaved family's house for a meal. Tracy was helping her mother by asking guests what kinds of drinks they wanted. She would approach small groups of adults and say, "Do you want coffee, lemonade, or Pepsi?" Then she would report back to the kitchen and fill the order. But she was startled when she approached one group of adults just as they burst out laughing. It made her angry that anyone could laugh when her father was dead.

Tracy ran crying to her room, saying, "People are laughing and having fun when my daddy is dead!" She was feeling angry and guilty, believing no one deserved to be happy anymore. Her mother and a friend had to convince her that the visitors *were* sad, but also had some happy thoughts; they needed to take turns between the sad and happy thoughts so they wouldn't get sick. They assured Tracy that her father would want her and the friends to have happy thoughts sometimes.

Tracy understood. Her grief did not become pathological. This is usually the case; there is generally a need for concern only when children display unusually delayed, distorted, or prolonged grief responses. The best way to help normally grieving children is to listen and care. As we spend time with them and reassure them, they will raise the questions that concern them most.

Fourth, *don't lie to children or use overly abstract explanations.* Often when parents lie or distort communication to children, they say they are doing it to protect the child. Usually they are protecting themselves and not helping the child.

When a child is told that a dead person "went on vacation," the child sometimes fears vacations and random abandonment. When someone says, "God loved this person so much that He took him to heaven," a child may fear God's love or an unpredictable death. When a child is told, "He fell asleep," he or she sometimes fears sleep and tries to stay awake. When someone says, "He died because he was sick," all sickness may seem life-threatening.

It helps a child when the actual causes of death are mentioned. A child can begin to discern between illnesses such as colds and measles, and terminal conditions such as cancer or heart attack.

Fifth, *consider the importance of rites of passage for children.* Rites of passage are familiar gestures which signal that major changes have taken place. Viewings, funerals, and interments are cultural ways to confront death and to signal the changes it brings. Good-bye visits, memory sessions, and cleaning out belongings are also ways to face the transitions.

A child who is seven or older and *wants* to attend some of these events should be allowed to do so; he needs to feel he is participating with the family. An adult should give him a clear advance explanation of what he will see and hear. It is also important that an adult accompany the child at all times during the rite of passage. If the child doesn't want to attend, there are other ways to confront the death. Sometimes a later graveside visit, viewing funeral photographs, or keeping an object related to the deceased helps a child focus on the reality of his loss.

How the Bible Can Help a Child Understand Death

Many Bible stories focus on the realities of aging, grief, and death. Parents can use them as they discuss these topics with their children. The death of Jesus Christ, for example, is a great model for death education; it permits discussion of physical death, burial, the presence of the spirit with God in heaven, and the idea of resurrection. While it is not advisable to dwell on the suffering of Christ with young children, the account does teach the concepts of spiritual redemption and the hope of resurrection. Any biblical account of healing or resurrection allows us and our children to look beyond sickness and death to God's power and eternal life.

The story of Jacob's death provides an opportunity to discuss the death of an elderly relative as well as the issue of funeral customs. If this story is used with children, they should be assured that their own parents are not dying now—that their parents will probably not die until the children are grown-up and have families of their own. Parents should also assure them that if they knew they were going to die soon, they would tell the children; the children don't have to fear a conspiracy of silence. It would also be wise to assure that if both parents died, the children would be kept together and loved in a familiar family. If there is a will, it can be explained in this context.

Any analogies used to explain death to children should emphasize transition over cessation, since there is an afterlife.[27] These analogies should also distinguish between the inner spiritual person and outer physical body; parents could use the analogy of a caterpillar changing into a butterfly, or a person moving out of a house and leaving it empty while moving into a new house.

Perhaps the best analogy is one the Apostle Paul used in the New Testament. Throughout 2 Corinthians 5 he uses the tent, a collapsible dwelling, as a symbol for the body. In 2 Timothy 4:6 he describes his coming death as a "departure." The original word stood for the collapsing of a tent or the breaking of camp.

A parent might tell the story of Paul and his death, using the tent analogy: "Many years ago there lived a man named Paul who was very old. He was a special servant of God. He was getting ready to die. He knew that he would be dead soon; God had told him that. He knew that his body would stop breathing. But he knew that the real Paul, who was inside the body, would go to live where God is.

"Paul thought back over his life and remembered the many times he had done God's work. He was pleased that he had obeyed God so many times, and felt as if he had just run a long race. He also felt as if he had just finished a long stay at school because he had learned so much. And he felt as if he had just fought a hard battle and won.

"In the Bible Paul said, 'It is time for me to leave.' He knew that when he got old and it was time to die, he would leave his body behind. Leaving is like taking down a tent; a tent can be full of life, fun, people, and noise, but sometimes we have to leave our tent and camping site. We don't always like that part of the camping trip. When we take all the fun things out of the tent, it is empty, quiet. Then we fold it up and put it away.

"When a person gets old like Paul was, God may say it is time to leave—to die. When a person dies, he leaves his body as we leave a tent. The body becomes empty, quiet, still, dead. We may not like to think about that ending part of life. The body is put in a box in the ground, just as we put a folded tent in its special place in the attic. But the real, *inside* person who laughs, thinks, cries, and remembers can go to be with Jesus in a happy place forever—in heaven. The real, inside person does not go into the ground; only the outside body does."

The Merry-Go-Round

Parents should offer their children a regular diet of healthy messages about life. I picture every loving parent as standing on a merry-go-round, trying to balance a child on his or her "horse." As the merry-go-round revolves, the child tends to lean too far to one side or the other. Without help, he might even fall off the horse and roll right off the ride.

Each revolution of this imaginary ride represents a day, week, month, or year in the life of that child. The alert parent can reassure the child and help him to enjoy the ride by pointing out some of the landmarks that keep passing in and out of view: There's the ticket booth, Grandma, the cotton-candy machine, the exit. Any child is fortunate to have at least one caring adult who will accompany him in life and point our again and again most of the familiar landmarks he will need.

One day that child will have to ride alone or stand beside other insecure little people who are just beginning their rides.

As a pastor and death educator I am concerned that parents translate life's landmarks into positive messages for their children. Parents who want to keep their children blind to life's realities until life forces them to do otherwise have forgotten something—that light is blinding to those who have been kept in darkness. As your children move through life, look for the many opportunities you will have to point out and *live* out some of the following landmark truths:

1. *Life does not stand still.* It is moving. There is a past, present, and future to every person's life. Celebrating birthdays, holidays, and anniversaries reminds us that life is progressing. We should be grateful to God for the lives we have.

2. *Everyone is aging.* All of us used to be younger than we are now. All of us will be older than we are now. As we age, we change. The differences caused by aging can be good or bad; some of them let us do things we couldn't before, while others keep us from doing things we could do before.

3. *It's OK to say the word "dead."* Many things in life don't live, move, breathe, stay warm, or make noise. Rocks are "dead," and so are nails. But some things are alive; they move, jump, breathe, make noise, and stay warm. We are alive. Sometimes plants, animals, and people become dead; they die.

4. *It's OK to be sad.* Sometimes we feel sad when we lose or break something special like a toy, when a pet dies, or when something changes. Whenever we like something a lot, we feel sad or angry when we lose it. It's OK to feel sad or to tell somebody else you feel sad. It's not OK to *hurt* another person or yourself just because you feel sad or angry. God always cares about you and understands how you feel when you lose something or someone.

5. *It's always hard to say good-bye to people or things we really like.* But if we love someone, we say good-bye even if it makes us feel sad. We say good-bye a lot of times in life—to people, things, places, and ideas. Saying good-bye means something has changed, and we have to keep on growing. Sometimes we're afraid that we will have to say good-bye to someone we care about or to something we like. It's OK to feel a little afraid; even adults feel that way sometimes. But God always

takes care of us and will never leave us. We need to do the things that are important before we have to say good-bye; we need to learn to say, "I love you. I'm sorry; will you forgive me? I need you; will you help me?"

Watch for Children's Anxieties about Death

Parents should be alert to natural anxiety about death; discussing the subject can cause uneasiness on the part of the adult *and* the child. But research shows that those who receive accurate information and personal support during this process can turn their uneasiness into calm. We are usually afraid of the unknown, not the known. Healthy death education helps us discover the known so that we can adjust to it.

At the same time, parents should not force-feed their children with death education. When the "merry-go-round" passes a landmark, point it out. Follow your child's natural curiosity; answer his or her questions with clarity, honesty, and security. Be genuine about your own feelings, and be factual; when you don't know the answers, admit it.

If your child's question triggers panic on your part, he will probably sense that his curiosity has touched a nerve. As a result he will tend to stay away from that subject and even begin to dread it. Thus *how* you answer is at least as important as *what* you answer.

When a landmark passes out of view and your child's curiosity about death is dormant, drop the subject. It will come up again. There is no need to create anxiety by leading children to think about their own deaths or the deaths of still-living parents or brothers and sisters. Unless these people are dying, children don't need to prematurely confront such major losses. Death should be discussed as something that usually happens to other people when they are older, and from natural causes. Only specific circumstances would dictate discussion of death as personal and intimate.

Teaching Children about Heaven

Christian parents should not hesitate to talk about the afterlife. Many death educators discourage the teaching of specific religious beliefs, but the Bible requires it. God looks to the family as the main teacher of such truths (Deut. 6:4-9).

When teaching a child about heaven, we should keep his or her value system in mind. Heaven is a place of rest, which might excite an elderly, tired person; but for children, heaven's happiness, beauty, and activity are its greatest attributes. In describing heaven, we should be careful not to exaggerate or sensationalize it. There is growing concern over the number of childhood "accidents" and suicides associated with fantasies. Instead, heaven can be described as a stark contrast to earth's realities—a place with no darkness or tears. Children who are terminally ill or handicapped will especially want to know about heaven. All children who have seen hearing aids, wheelchairs, and eyeglasses can appreciate the fact that there is no sickness, sorrow, or death in heaven.

Every believing adult who loves children should be prepared to present the Gospel to them. Believing in Christ is the qualification for entrance into heaven; one sound way to present this idea to a child is to use the passport analogy. Such a presentation might sound like this: "Did you ever travel to another country? When we travel from one country to another, we need a special piece of paper called a passport. When you walk, drive, fly, or sail into another country, the people there will ask to see your special piece of paper. If you have the passport, they will say, 'Come in!' If you do not have the passport, they will say, 'Sorry, you can't come in!'

"When someone dies—when God says it is time for that person's body to stop working and eating and drinking and breathing—that person flies away from his body like a butterfly flies from its cocoon or a family moves away from its old house. The person takes a short, fast trip from here to heaven—from earth to where Jesus is. When he arrives at heaven, the person finds that it is like a beautiful new country. Someone will say, 'Should we let him in? Does he have his passport?'

"Then the person can say, 'Yes. I can come in. I have my passport. I believe in Jesus. I asked Jesus to forgive the wrong things I've done. I asked Jesus to live in me. I can come into heaven.' Everyone will be happy—the person, his family, his friends, Jesus, and the angels. The real, *inside* person will live in heaven forever. His new body will be beautiful and he'll never have any problems with it. He will be happy there with his friends, family, and Jesus."

Parents can enlarge on any part of the passport analogy as they feel it necessary. Parents who are sensitive to the way children view things will want to follow guidelines like these and use them to equip their children for life as well as death.

12

Search for Tomorrow

In the words of the infamous soap opera, we are all in a "search for tomorrow." Our society seems desperate to know the future. People by the thousands consult astrology for supposed glimpses into their tomorrows; interest in all forms of prophecy has skyrocketed; scientists are trying to project our global futures regarding ecology, economics, and political conflict.

Nuclear buildup and nuclear disarmament are both proposed out of fear of an undesirable future. Medicine is stepping up its attack on disease, aging, and even death in an effort to control personal futures. Science fiction is doing a booming business, touching a nerve that is anxious about the future; universities are dramatically increasing their programs in futurology (future studies), gerontology (the study of aging), and thanatology (the study of death). Every bookstore's shelves illustrate the popular demand to know the future, and every news report touches on the fear of what could happen next—personally, nationally, and as a race.

People commonly respond in one of three ways to this pressure to know the future. Two responses are inadequate and unhealthy; the third is biblical and wholesome.

#1: The Rigid Controller
The Rigid Controller says by his words or actions, "I am going to take things into my own hands. I will personally guarantee

111

my future." This person scans the horizon for variables that will affect him in the future, such as illness, age, poverty, and physical danger. Once he has identified his enemies, he engineers his life into a hyperactive attempt to control them.

The Rigid Controller often launches unceasing attempts to stay financially or physically fit. He also finds himself trying to mask the steady aging process. Cosmetics, clothing, and even lifestyle choices shout, "I'm not getting old!" When the Rigid Controller thinks in dollar signs, he commits himself to money-making and money-saving plans that he hopes will enlarge his retirement nest egg to great proportions.

I met a Rigid Controller. He was a brilliant man with a doctorate in chemistry. But he was also a fearful and pessimistic man. He had spent several years planning and building an "Armageddon retreat"—a wilderness mountain refuge where he could flee once the inevitable collapse of civilized society had taken place. His Armageddon retreat was at a rural site two hours outside New York City. Though he lived and worked in the city, this scientist believed a survival bunker could only be built in the remote mountains.

This man could control microscopic chemical reactions, but he couldn't control his fear. Every day he found "proof" that the country was on the verge of economic collapse, and that civilization would soon explode in a nuclear mushroom. Only those who could rush to their underground cement houses could find water and preserved food which would be uncontaminated by nuclear fallout. Gold stored there would provide bartering power among the holocaust survivors; weapons would provide law and order. But the sad reality is that even if this man were to survive an attack through his elaborate self-preservation scheme, he would still be the same man—rigid, controlling, fearful.

The Apostle James warns of the dangers of being a Rigid Controller (James 4:13-17). He confronts a group of commercial schemers–self-confident merchants who behave as though the future were subject to their calculations. He condemns them for their boastful pride, their unjust treatment of laborers (5:4, 6), and their prejudice against poor people (2:1-9).[28]

James assaults these Rigid Controllers with truth: "Not only can't you manage the future, you can't even manage your own lives! Your lives are like smoke, like puffs of steam" (4:14, author's paraphrase). Their greatest business assets, their lives, could evaporate in an instant. Their amassed possessions would last only long enough to serve as fuel in God's fiery judgment (5:1-3, 5). They would become like flowers that fade quickly under the scorching sun (1:10-11).

To heed James' warnings, we should acknowledge how rapidly our lives could change. In a matter of moments we could lose our health or our jobs, or face family or national crises. Such radical changes happen to good and bad, young and old.

I have been reminded of this many times—perhaps never with more shock than when I arrived too late at the scene of a fight between two teenage boys at a Christian camp. In an instant of unsupervised time, one of the boys was paralyzed from the neck down through the angry aggression of another camper. Neither boy's life would ever be the same.

James challenges his hearers to recognize that physical life is temporary. He urges them to include an element of dependence on God in all their plans. He insists that all people, rich and poor, should wait patiently and hopefully for the Lord to return (5:7-8).

The Deaf Ignorer

While the Rigid Controller confronts the future and tries to control it, the Deaf Ignorer denies the future and pretends he can stay in the present.

Peter spoke out against the Deaf Ignorers of his day. These people laughed at the Christian view of the future: "Where is the promise of His coming? For ever since the fathers fell asleep, all continues just as it was from the beginning of creation" (2 Peter 3:4). They rejected the notions of Christ's return, personal judgment after death, world renovation, and the establishment of Christ's kingdom on earth. They tried to live in an eternal present.

Deaf Ignorers demand immediate gratification. They can't be bothered with thinking about long-distant future events. For all practical purposes, events which can't be proved to their immediate satisfaction will never happen. The natural result of such a philosophy is indulgence and self-gratification. It is this theme of lustful self-gratification which Peter confronts among the Deaf Ignorers (2 Peter 1:4; 2:1-3, 10, 13-14, 18, 22).

Peter also exhorts the Christian to be attentive to the future (2 Peter 3:12); to have a holy lifestyle rather than a self-gratifying one; and to believe in Christ's return, judgment, and kingdom, even though these realities are not yet physically present. It is precisely this concept of deferred gratification or future reward that is intended to encourage the Christian who is undergoing suffering and persecution (1 Peter 1:6-7). This belief in future, higher judgment allows a believer to persevere and submit to unjust and lower authorities now.

Deaf Ignorers in Peter's day and in ours follow the old Epicurean philosophy, "Eat, drink, and be merry, for tomorrow we die." For these people death is not the entrance to eternity or the gateway to judgment; it is extinction. The natural consequence of such a philosophy is to satiate oneself with pleasure—unbridled sex, food, drink, ego, luxury, personal ease, and gratification. As the TV commercial says, "You only go around once in life, so grab for all the gusto you can!" Many live this way, deaf to the realities of the future.

John Dillinger, the first millionaire bank robber, exemplified this indulgent lifestyle. His existence was one of constant self-gratification as he tried to ignore his inevitable future of punishment and death. How did his life end? Prematurely, at the hands of FBI agents. Dillinger died with thirty-two cents in his pocket.[29]

The Responsible Pilgrim

How should the Bible-believing Christian face life now and in the future? Should he try to postpone his self-gratification into an earthly future, as the Rigid Controller does? Should he try to cram all of his pleasure into an earthly present, as does the Deaf Ignorer? On the contrary, he should approach life as a Responsible Pilgrim (1 Peter 2:11).

While the Responsible Pilgrim should plan for the future, he must not do it in the God-excluding, earthbound mode of the Rigid Controller. While he should experience some God-given pleasures now, he must not do so in the unbridled, self-indulgent manner of the Deaf Ignorer.

Paul wrote from prison, "Our citizenship is in heaven, from which also we eagerly wait for a Saviour, the Lord Jesus Christ; who will transform the body of our humble state into conformity with the body of His glory" (Phil. 3:20-21). With this in mind, how does the Responsible Pilgrim think and act?

1. *He knows that the best kind of life, now and in the future, is centered in Christ.* The Christian's fulfillment cannot be found in financial security or materialism; the deepest pleasures come in giving, not receiving. Real life is found in a relationship to the Saviour. He came saying, "I came that they might have life, and might have it abundantly" (John 10:10). The tragedy is that most of us do not consider Christ's lifestyle worth living; it is too risky and "laid back" for the Rigid Controller because it is a life of faith—too "boring" and stoic for the Deaf Ignorer because it is a life of discipline.

One of Christ's great Responsible Pilgrims, the Apostle Paul, said, "For to me, to live is Christ, and to die is gain" (Phil. 1:21). He wasn't obsessed with physical survival or spiritualist escapism. He had learned to be content with the will of God whether it meant life or death, hardship or ease. For Paul, life's goal was "that I may know Him" (Phil. 3:10). The hopes and dreams on which our minds dwell will likely reveal whether we are responsible sojourners in the footsteps of Jesus.

2. *The Responsible Pilgrim accepts the limitations of earthly life while still anticipating the blessedness of heavenly life.* Paul accepted the realities of prison and a misunderstood ministry while looking forward to life with Christ after death (Phil. 1:12-26). He knew that through trials the Lord reminds us not to sink our roots too deeply into earthly soil.

Think back to your last trial—the last time you were stopped by trouble. Maybe your car broke down or your well-made plans were changed. You probably felt a normal surge of emotion. But how did you respond after the initial feeling? Did you get stuck in anger? Did your sadness turn into paralyzing depression? Faith in God allows you the creativity of reframing your troubles as a joyful training process (James 1:2-4). Confidence in God's ultimate purpose permits you to reach out for His holiness and peace (Heb. 12:10-11).

3. *The Responsible Pilgrim accepts God's promises and lives by them.* Abraham, like most of us, had become attached to his

homeland and relatives. But God told Abraham to leave these attachments and go to a land he had never seen. His only connection to this place was God's promise. Was God reliable enough for Abraham to risk security for an invisible Promised Land? Abraham believed He was, and began a real-life spiritual quest. Against all odds, he was a Responsible Pilgrim (Heb. 11:8-10).

Peter was a missionary in New Guinea. His work among jungle tribesmen often kept him away from his wife and children for days at a time. While Peter was gone on one such trek, his youngest son came down with a dangerously high fever. Because there was no medical help available, the son had to try to outlast the fever for three days. He survived—but with serious brain damage that would affect him for life.

Peter had a choice: would he believe God's call to New Guinea had been good? (1 Thes. 5:24) Would he believe that this mental defect would work together for good? (Rom. 8:28) Peter chose to believe. Twenty years later he is firmly persuaded that God called him to New Guinea and permitted this injury for some secret and eternal glory yet to be revealed. Peter is a Responsible Pilgrim.

4. *The Responsible Pilgrim makes reasonable plans for the future which are profitable according to the Word of God.* Though Paul would have liked nothing more than to stand before Christ, he used his time and abilities wisely on earth. He preached in the larger cities first, then to the Jewish community, seeing the value of reaching population centers and those who had an Old Testament background like his. He didn't spend his time waiting for Christ's return or for some miraculous revelation about what he should do. He made plans for his future which agreed with the values of God's Word. He lived a useful present life with confident future plans (Acts 13-14).

5. *The Responsible Pilgrim is open to the way God may change his plans.* Though Paul based most of his plans on spiritual common sense, he was also open to special guidance from the Lord (Acts 16:9-10). While on his second missionary journey, Paul saw a miraculous vision through which the Lord shifted his plans. The Rigid Controller could never accept God's spontaneous rearranging; the Deaf Ignorer would make no plans to start with; but Paul struck a balance of careful

116

planning and spiritual sensitivity.

6. *The Responsible Pilgrim does not worry about the future.* Rather he realizes that God knows his future and is trustworthy. Just as God dresses the lilies and feeds the birds without any anxiety on their part, He frees us from constant preoccupation with providing for our futures (Matt. 6:19-34). How often we find ourselves obsessed with the future; instead we are to do the work God has given us and cast all our anxieties on Him (1 Peter 5:7).

7. *The Responsible Pilgrim sees this life as temporary and patiently waits for the Lord to come back.* According to James, believers of every age and financial bracket should live in light of our Lord's eventual return (James 4:13–5:8).

8. *The Responsible Pilgrim lives a holy, enduring lifestyle oriented toward Christ's return, judgment, and kingdom.* The Christian life is not only the best way to live now; it also lays a foundation for eternity (2 Peter 3:8-13). We must not trade God's great truths for earth's meager fads. The pain we may suffer for saying yes to God's way and no to the wrong things may seem unending, but will eventually be replaced by joy. The early Christians, who were threatened and often martyred, knew this. One of their early, inspired hymns went like this:

For if we died with Him, we shall also live with Him;
If we endure, we shall also reign with Him;
If we deny Him, He also will deny us;
If we are faithless, He remains faithful;
For He cannot deny Himself (2 Tim. 2:11-13).

9. *The Responsible Pilgrim anticipates a radical change in the world and in himself at the return of Christ.* The good news is that the world's pattern of sin and deterioration will be interrupted one day. God will liberate the earth from the curse of sin (Rom. 8:18-23). Murder, rape, war, aging, and death will end; we will also be changed.

The Apostle John was delighted that we are God's children (1 John 3:1-3), and that we will someday be more like Christ. Though he could not articulate what we will be like when we are changed, he knew that the change will be good: "Beloved, now we are children of God, and it has not appeared as yet what we shall be. We know that, when He appears, we shall be like Him, because we shall see Him just as He is. And everyone who has this hope fixed on Him purifies himself just as He is pure" (1 John 3:2-3).

The benefits of living as a Responsible Pilgrim are numerous and profound. There is the deep satisfaction of obedience, and freedom from anxiety as we face the future. This freedom allows us to be generous because we know God will take care of us. Pilgrim living also frees us to enjoy modest pleasures rather than requiring extravagance.

As Jonathan Edwards prayed, "May we live in such a way as we shall wish we had lived when we stand before Him."

13

The Future Is Now

A few years ago the zealous head coach of the Washington Redskins football team declared his motto: "The Future Is Now!" To some it seemed contradictory; how could the *future* be *now?* But we long-time Redskin fans knew exactly what he meant. Those dreams of post-season play, championships, and the Super Bowl were no longer to be projected into the "sometime distant future." Those opportunities were here, within our grasp, available to us in the present.

Solomon Looks at the Present and Future

As noted in chapter 9, the wise King Solomon had much to say about old age. But he had more to say about the whole of life and the fact that "the future is now." In Ecclesiastes 12:1 he wrote, "Remember also your Creator in the days of your youth, before the evil days come and the years draw near when you will say, 'I have no delight in them.'" He was saying, "Don't see old age and death as far-off, as a remote and unreal possibility." He was exhorting his readers to take action now, to seize opportunities today to influence those "distant" events.

Whether we *feel* older or not, our biological clocks are running steadily. Our ability to cope with our futures is built largely on the way we handle our todays. Our responses to God throughout life greatly influence our ability to maintain a healthy outlook in our final years.

One man who wishes he had followed Solomon's advice is named Matt. As a young man Matt lived dangerously, always seeking bigger and better thrills. But he also tried to find security and play some conservative options, working hard at his sales position and starting a family. By mid-life he had established a dual lifestyle as troubled alcoholic, gambler, roving romancer, successful entrepreneur, company vice president, and wealthy urbanite. He was a confusing mixture of wise and foolish choices.

Before his sixtieth birthday, however, Matt changed his ways He stopped drinking and gambling since those habits had caused him a major career crash. The family he had split was now communicating. His health improved. His explanation: "If I had known I was going to live this long I would have taken better care of my body. But I am living smarter now. . . . I am living the Christian life and am working an honest day's work for an honest day's wage. My advice to anyone is, 'start living smarter younger.' "

Wisdom and Folly

At the outset of the Book of Ecclesiastes, the aged philosopher Solomon acknowledges that he, like Matt, had pursued both wisdom and folly (1:17). As a young man he had determined to taste every fruit and walk every path. He had pursued the traditional Hebrew wisdom of the Bible as well as the unorthodox and radical views of skeptics in his day.[30] Thus Ecclesiastes 1–11 is his life story, a constant alternation between valid perspectives and empty ones.

As Solomon describes his life through this dual track philosophic monologue, he often introduces his more melancholy comments with, "I said to myself" (1:16; 2:1, 15; 3:17-18, etc.). These introductions indicate that we are hearing one of the earlier, foolish perspectives that had once been his. Often he follows this melancholy self-report with a corrective bit of wisdom.

This alternation between melancholy satire and wisdom has challenged readers' patience and powers of interpretation for centuries. But some of the greatest philosophers, authors, and politicians have been most effective when mixing satire with affirmative counsel. C.S. Lewis, for example, contributed greatly to coming generations through the melancholy satire of *A Grief Observed* (Bantam Books, 1976). In this little book he questions the unquestionable, challenging God for taking his wife of only a few years. Lewis demands to know why God would bring him "out of his shell" only to thrust him "back into the shell again." Lewis felt so uneasy about the satirical element of his book that he insisted it be published at first under a pseudonym. He felt that such unresolved grief and satire bordered on the irreverent. But it reflected his mood and experience in much the same way that Solomon's writing did.

Chasing Wind

Solomon tells us that pursuing folly is an empty adventure. It leads to vanishing mirages, deceptive shadows. It is like "striving after wind" (1:17).

When I was a child, every fall we would rake dry leaves and play in them. We would jump into them, bury each other in them, and ride our bikes through them. Often a gust of wind would rustle through the leaves, lifting a dozen or so into a swirling flurry. We would run after these little whirlwinds, never catching one. No matter how close we came, these flurries would elude our grasp or dissolve into just another pile of leaves. That's what chasing wind is like.

How often Solomon must have regretted this wind-chasing once he reached old age! How often *we* live as though we had forever to experiment with life, to play out the options and pay the banker later. Solomon wants us to see the urgency of our futures now, and to live today in light of tomorrow.

What's the Difference?

Several key sayings in Ecclesiastes reflect Solomon's satire of the cynical, self-serving frame of mind. At one point he declares that it doesn't matter how we live; since all people die and are forgotten, it doesn't really matter whether we've lived wisely or foolishly (2:16). Later he argues that humans and animals are the same. God made them to live by their instincts and to be destroyed in death, so there is no unique potential, moral accountability, or afterlife for the human being (3:17-22).

This way of thinking was common among skeptics in Solomon's day and is in ours. Many people adopt a value system that rejects absolute standards of right and wrong, looking instead for whatever makes them or the greatest number of other people feel good. Accepting this rationalization could permit almost any crime, as it did when the Nazis believed that exterminating the Jews was ethical. The adage, "Let your conscience be your guide," is only as good as one's conscience. God will judge us according to whether our actions and consciences were attuned to His absolute standards (12:13-14).

At another point Solomon satirically says that it is better to be dead than alive. At least the dead don't feel pain and injustice as the living do (4:2-3). To those who labor diligently, Solomon cries, "Why bother?" Each of us was born naked and poor; this is always our fate in death. We can't take anything with us (5:15-16).

Though Solomon saw death as a wretched evil, there was one thing worse than death—a manipulative and seductive woman (7:26). She is as good to a man as poison is. Then Solomon says that man cannot know or influence the time of his death (8:8). He is but a spectator in the drama of his own life.

Finally Solomon turns the tables, declaring that it is better to be alive at all costs (9:4). He would rather be a dog (a symbol of a Gentile) who is alive and scavenging than to be a dignified but dead lion (a symbol of an entombed Judahite King).

The Bright Side

Interspersed throughout these satirical episodes, Solomon does dispense wisdom about aging and death. He maintains that we should learn to find contentment in what God has given us; when a person's basic physical needs are met and he can labor with simple dignity, this is ample reason for contentment before God (2:24-26). This advice contrasts with the folly of gluttony and cynicism about work (2:1, 3; 5:16).

Solomon would also have us recognize that death is like birth—it comes as part of a normal life cycle in its appropriate time (3:2). This attitude contrasts the pessimism and fatalism of 4:2-3 and 8:8.

He further encourages readers to enjoy their families. Since life is short we should maximize the deepest satisfaction of loving and being loved (9:9), being careful not to sacrifice family life on the altar of workaholism or the pursuit of a higher standard of living. This perspective refutes the death wish of 4:2-3 and the bitterness of relationships in 7:26.

Solomon wisely challenges his readers to share their possessions while they are still alive to enjoy them (11:2). He advises generosity rather than materialism (2:8). One wise middle-age couple gave a lot of thought to the way God wanted them to handle the inheritances their children and grandchildren would receive. They framed their conclusion in the following rhyme:

"Do your giving while you are living.
Then you'll be knowing where it is going."

This couple advised other parents to help young adult children when help was needed most—when children were getting their own families established, if possible. They knew the pleasure of seeing money help a loved one.

Coming to a Good End

After tracing the pendulum swings between wisdom and folly, Solomon reaffirms the wisdom of remembering and obeying God throughout life (12:1, 13-14). He builds a life-tested case for integrating the reality of old age and death into our current worldview. We are not to become morbidly preoccupied with death, but should allow our creaturely limitations to motivate us to root our lives in God, our Creator.

I knew a man who exemplified this truth. Wayne was 30 years old. He had a beautiful wife, two happy daughters, and a son on the way. His faith in Christ was genuine and deep; at work and in his extended family Wayne had built a clear testimony of his walk with the Lord. He was well liked by the staff at Lahey Clinic where he worked and witnessed to God's goodness.

It was time for Wayne's annual medical checkup at work, so he went through a routine examination with the company physician. As the doctor completed the exam, he asked Wayne,

"Do you have any pains, problems, or questions for me?"

"Well, I do have a bruise on my foot that doesn't seem to be going away," Wayne said. "And I feel very tired these days." These symptoms prompted further tests and a tragic diagnosis: leukemia.

The prognosis was that within a year Wayne would be dead. Chemotherapy would help temporarily, and the possibility of bone marrow transplants would give powerful but fading hope. Wayne would witness the birth of his third child, but if the prognosis was correct the baby would never remember him.

Physical death was coming to Wayne. The historic and divine consequence of Adam's sin had touched my friend. Yet Wayne constantly showed his belief that God was in control, even in control of leukemia. He was convinced his pain would soon give way to glory; in heaven there would be no sorrow, tears, or death.

Some of the doctors and nurses who cared for Wayne that year showed more fear and anxiety than he did. The Lord Jesus had conquered the fear of death for Wayne. What a pulpit he had that year from which to preach the Good News! From his hospital bed he demonstrated emotional balance and biblical wisdom as he explained the issues of spiritual life and death to visitors and hospital staff alike.

Wayne and his loved ones were honest about their grief. Life was painful; their feelings swung back and forth. There was grief for Wayne, for his eventual widow, and for their fatherless children. But they knew God understood their grief.

Wayne had learned of God's care years before when his father and brother had died, and when he had survived a bout with cancer as a teenager. This earlier cancer had been detected after an aggressive hockey player had angrily speared Wayne in a game; the injury exposed a growing cancer that probably would have gone undetected for some time. The other player had meant the injury for evil, but God had meant it for good; the early diagnosis had likely given him at least another decade of life for the Lord.

But this time there was to be no extension. The prognosis was correct; Wayne died just months after his new son was born.

Wayne had been a responsible pilgrim in life and in death.

Christ had become his spiritual companion, supporting him in times of need, allowing him to grow powerfully and testify effectively through his suffering. Christ had also given Wayne and his wife grace and wisdom to communicate openly with their children during this crisis. They demonstrated deep spiritual hope to everyone.

Wayne's example exhorts all of us to look beyond the fear so many associate with suffering and death. In the strength of Wayne's Lord, we can make the most of our short earthly lives—and face death honestly and hopefully.

NOTES

1. H.K. Congdon, *The Pursuit of Death* (Nashville: Abingdon, 1977), 10.
2. L. Bailey, *Biblical Perspectives on Death* (Philadelphia: Fortress, 1979), 75-85.
3. Catherine Marshall, editor, *John Doe, Disciple: Sermons for the Young in Heart* (New York: McGraw-Hill, 1963), 219-220.
4. L.R. Bailey, *Biblical Perspectives on Death* (Philadelphia: Fortress, 1979, 7-16.
5. J. Landorf, *Mourning Song* (Santa Ana, Calif.: One Way Cassette Library, 1975).
6. David O. Moberg, "Dealing with the Dying," *Christianity Today*, Apr. 23, 1982, 52-54.
7. Raymond A. Moody, Jr., *Life after Life* (Harrisburg, Pa.: Stackpole, 1976), 89.
8. Carlson Wade, *Yes! There's Life after Death* (Burbank, Calif.: Globe, 1982); Elisabeth Kubler-Ross, *Remember the Secret* (Millbrae, Calif.: Celestial Arts, 1982).
9. P. Bardis, *History of Thanatology* (Washington, D.C.: University Press of America, 1981), 37.
10. B. Schoenberg, A. Carr, D. Peretz, A. Kutscher, editors, *Loss and Grief: Psychological Management in Medical Practice* (New York: Columbia, 1970), 3-19.
11. E. Kubler-Ross, *On Death and Dying* (New York: MacMillan, 1969), 38-137.
12. W.M. Chandler, *The Trial of Jesus*, 2 vols. (Atlanta: Harrison, 1908) 98-99.
13. C. Swindoll, *For Those Who Hurt* (Portland: Multnomah, 1977), 8, 10.
14. E. Grollman, *Suicide* (Boston: Beacon, 1971), 72.
15. J. Bayly, *The View from a Hearse* (Elgin, Ill.: D.C. Cook, 1969), 74.

16. J.F. Childress, *Priorities in Biomedical Ethics* (Philadelphia: Westminster, 1981), 34-50; P.D. Simmons, *Birth and Death: Bioethical Decision-Making* (Philadelphia: Westminster, 1983), 107-154.
17. J.A. Fruehling, editor, *Sourcebook on Death and Dying*, first edition (Chicago: Marquis, 1982), 288-296.
18. C. Ryrie, *The Ryrie Study Bible* (Chicago: Moody, 1976, 1978), 957-958.
19. Bert Kruger Smith, *Aging in America* (Boston: Beacon, 1973).
20. Judith Stevens-Long, *Adult Life—Developmental Processes* (Palo Alto, Calif.: Mayfield, 1979), 360.
21. J.K. Anderson, *Life, Death, and Beyond* (Grand Rapids: Zondervan, 1980), 112; W. Bradbury, *Into the Unknown* (Pleasantville, N.Y.: Reader's Digest Assoc., Inc., 1981), 272; T. Brooke, *The Other Side of Death* (Wheaton, Ill.: Tyndale, 1979), 33-49; R.A. Moody, *Life after Death* (Harrisburg, Pa. Stackpole, 1976), 41-56; M.S. Rawlings, *Before Death Comes* (Nashville: Nelson, 1980), 44-45; P.J. Swihart, *The Edge of Death* (Downer's Grove, Ill.: InterVarsity, 1978), 15-16.
22. R.B.Y. Scott, *Proverbs-Ecclesiastes* in *The Anchor Bible* (vol. 18), W.F. Albright, D.N. Freedman, editors (Garden City, N.Y.: Doubleday, 1964), 254-255.
23. E. Kubler-Ross, "Reactions to the Seminar on Death and Dying," in *On Death and Dying* (New York: MacMillan, 1969), 265-266; Cicely Saunders, "St. Christopher's Hospice," in E.S. Schneidman, editor, *Death: Current Perspectives*, second edition (Palo Alto, Calif.: Mayfield, 1976), 356-357.
24. C. Gordon, "Nuzu Tablets," in E.F. Campbell, editor, *Biblical Archaeologist Reader*, third edition (Garden City, N. Y.: Doubleday, 1970), 28; K. Kitchen, *Ancient Orient and the Old Testament* (Downer's Grove, Ill.: InterVarsity, 1966), 128; E. Speiser, *Genesis* in *The Anchor Bible* (vol. 1), W.F. Albright, D. N. Freedman, editors (Garden City, N.Y.: Doubleday, 1964), 370.
25. J.J. Davis, *Paradise to Prison* (Grand Rapids: Baker, 1975), 301-303; Manuel Komroff, editor, *The History of Herodotus*, trans. G. Rawlinson (New York: Tudor, 1939), 108; N. Sarna, *Understanding Genesis* (New York: Jewish Theological Seminary, 1966), 226; and J.M. Freeman, *Manners and Customs of the Bible* (Plainfield, N.J.: Logos, 1972), 15, 43, 46, 49, 55, 57-59.
26. See E. Grollman, *Talking about Death* (Boston: Beacon, 1970), XI-XIII; by the same author, *Explaining Death to Children* (Boston: Beacon, 1967), 241-279; R. Kopp, *Where Has Grandpa Gone?* (Grand Rapids: Zondervan, 1983).
27. Moving from house to house in J. Bayly, "The Christian Attitude to Death" (Vancouver, B.C.: Regent College Tape #203B); passport and traveling by Handi°vangelism ministry of Bible Club Movement (Upper Darby, Pa., 1983); butterfly and cocoon in E. Kubler-Ross, "Life, Death, and Life after Death" (cassette #1, Escondido, Calif.: Shanti Nilaya, 1980).
28. Bo Reicke, *The Epistles of James, Peter, and Jude* in *The Anchor Bible* (vol. 37), W.F. Albright, D.N. Freedman, editors (Garden City, N.Y.:

Doubleday, 1964), 48-49.

29. Anthony Campolo, Jr., *The Success Fantasy* (Wheaton Ill Victor, 1980), 12.

30. R.B.Y. Scott, *Proverbs-Ecclesiastes* in *The Anchor Bible* (vol 18) W.F. Albright, D.N. Freedman, editors (Garden City, N.Y.: Doubleday, 1964), 212-213; F. Delitzsch, *Proverbs, Ecclesiastes, Song of Solomon* in *Commentary on the Old Testament* (vol. VI), trans. J. Martin, C.F. Keil, F. Delitzsch, editors (Grand Rapids: Eerdmans, 1872), 230-231.

FOR FURTHER READING

Aging

J. Gillies, *A Guide to Caring for and Coping with Aging Parents* (Nashville: Nelson, 1981).

H. Vander Lugt, *The Art of Growing Old* (Grand Rapids: Radio Bible Class, 1980).

J. Stevens-Long, *Adult Life—Developmental Processes* (Palo Alto, Calif.: Mayfield, 1939).

The Christian's Personal Future

G. Friesen, *Decision Making and the Will of God* (Portland: Multnomah, 1980).

D. Winter, *Hereafter* (Wheaton, Ill.: Shaw, 1972).

Educational Thanatology

G. Mills, *et al*, *Discussing Death: A Guide to Death Education* (Palm Springs, Calif.: ETC Publications, 1982).

H. Wass, *et al*, *Death Education: An Annotated Resource Guide* (New York: Hemisphere, 1980).

For Children

L. Buscaglia, *The Fall of Freddie the Leaf* (Thorofare, N.J.: Slack, 1982).

L. Chandler, *Uncle Ike* (Nashville: Broadman, 1981).

E. Grollman, *Talking about Death—A Dialogue between Parent and Child* (Boston: Beacon, 1970).

C. Nystrom, *What Happens When We Die?* (Chicago: Moody, 1981).

E. Roberts, *Heaven Has a Floor* (New York: Damascus, 1979).

P. White, *What's Happened to Auntie Jean?* (Glendale, Calif.: Regal, 1976).

For Those Who Communicate with Children

E. Grollman, *Explaining Death to Children* (Boston: Beacon, 1967).

R. Kopp, *Where Has Grandpa Gone?* (Grand Rapids: Zondervan, 1983).

H. Schiff, *The Bereaved Parent* (New York: Penguin, 1977).

Grief

R. Bailey, *Ministering to the Grieving* (Grand Rapids: Zondervan, 1976).

P. Barnhart, *Devotions for Patients* (Old Tappan, N.J.: Revell, 1983).

J. Landorf, *Mourning Song* (Old Tappan, N.J.: Revell, 1974).

Historical Thanatology

P. Bardis, *History of Thanatology* (Washington, D.C.: University Press of America, 1981).

E.A.W. Budge, *Osiris and the Egyptian Resurrection* (New York: Dover, 1911).

N. Davies, *Human Sacrifice in History and Today* (New York: Morrow, 1981).

M. Eliade, *Death, Afterlife, and Eschatology* (New York: Harper, 1967).

Jesus' Death

W. Chandler, *The Trial of Jesus* (Atlanta: Harrison, 1908).

N. Douty, *The Death of Christ* (Swengel, Pa.: Reiner, 1972).

H. Ridderbos, *Paul—An Outline of His Theology* (Grand Rapids: Eerdmans, 1975).

Medical Thanatology

J.F. Childress, *Priorities in Biomedical Ethics* (Philadelphia: Westminster, 1981).

J. Ewens and P. Herrington, *Hospice* (Santa Fe: Bear, 1982).

M. Hamilton and H. Reid, *A Hospice Handbook* (Grand Rapids: Eerdmans, 1980).

E. Kubler-Ross, *On Death and Dying* (New York: MacMillan, 1969).

P. Rossman, *Hospice* (New York: Fawcett Columbine, 1977).

B. Schoenberg, *et al*, *Loss and Grief: Psychological Management in Medical Practice* (New York: Columbia, 1970).

P. Simmons, *Birth and Death: Bioethical Decision-Making* (Philadelphia: Westminster, 1983).

Parapsychology

J.K. Anderson, *Life, Death, and Beyond* (Grand Rapids: Zondervan, 1980).

T. Brooke, *The Other Side of Death* (Wheaton, Ill.: Tyndale, 1979).

M. Rawlings, *Before Death Comes* (Nashville: Nelson, 1980).

P. Swihart, *The Edge of Death* (Downer's Grove, Ill.: InterVarsity, 1978).

Postmortem Facts

D. Dempsey, *The Way We Die* (New York: McGraw-Hill, 1975).

R. Shipley, *The Consumer's Guide to Death, Dying, and Bereavement* (Palm Springs, Calif.: ETC Publications, 1982).

Religious Thanatology

L. Bailey, *Biblical Perspectives on Death* (Phildelphia: Fortress, 1979).

R. Kopp, *Encounter with Terminal Illness* (Grand Rapids: Zondervan, 1980).

L. Richards and P. Johnson, *Death and the Caring Community* (Portland: Multnomah, 1980).

H. Stone, *The Caring Church* (New York: Harper, 1983).

Suffering

J. Claypool, *Tracks of a Fellow Struggler* (Waco, Tex.: Word, 1974).

J. Wenham, *The Goodness of God* (Downer's Grove, Ill.: InterVarsity, 1974).

P. Yancey, *Where Is God When It Hurts?* (Grand Rapids: Zondervan, 1979).

Suicide

J. Bailey, *The View from a Hearse* (Elgin, Ill.: D.C. Cook, 1969).

E. Grollman, *Suicide* (Boston: Beacon, 1971).